Canada in the Atlantic Economy

T0316790

CANADA IN THE ATLANTIC ECONOMY

Published:

Forthcoming:

Canadian Economic Policy and the Impact of International Capital Flows

Richard E. Caves, Grant L. Reuber

Published for the
Private Planning Association of Canada by University of Toronto Press

To William B. Lambert

These studies of "Canada in the Atlantic Economy" are dedicated with respect and gratitude to the late William B. Lambert, Chairman of the Board of the Private Planning Association of Canada from 1965 to 1967, who played a vital role in the development and supervision of the Atlantic Economic Studies Program, on which the publications are based.

His interest went far beyond his formal responsibility; he held a deep conviction concerning the importance of international cooperation among the North Atlantic nations. His untimely death came when the first draft studies had entered the early stages of publication.

© University of Toronto Press 1969 / Reprinted 2015 / ISBN 978-0-8020-3244-7 (pap

This study was prepared concurrently with a longer version, *Capital Transfers and Economic Policy: Canada, 1951–1962*, by Richard E. Caves and Grant L. Reuber, with R. W. Baguley, J. M. Curtis, and R. Lubitz, which will be published in 1970 by Harvard University Press.

Foreword

There have been two outstanding developments in international trade policy during the past twenty years—the multilateral dismantling of trade barriers under the General Agreement on Tariffs and Trade, which has been the agency for several rounds of successful tariff negotiations since its inception in 1947, and the establishment of the European Economic Community and the European Free Trade Association in the late 1950s. In a period of reconstruction and then sustained growth, these policies have helped the participating nations of the Atlantic area to experience the benefits of internation specialization and expanding trade. The wealth generated by trade and domestic prosperity has also made possible external aid programs to assist economic growth in the developing countries.

Whatever the trade and economic development problems of the future, it is widely acknowledged that the industrially advanced countries of the North Atlantic region must play an important role. It is also generally conceded that the ability of these countries to maintain their own economic growth and prosperity and to contribute to that of the less advanced nations will be greatly enhanced if they can reduce or remove the remaining trade barriers among themselves. Cooperation among Atlantic countries is now fostered by the GATT and by the Organisation for Economic Co-operation and Development. But the success of these and other approaches depends on the assessment by each country of the importance of international trade liberalization and policy coordination for its domestic economy and other national interests. This is particularly true for countries such as Canada which are heavily dependent upon export markets.

The Atlantic Economic Studies Program of the Private Planning Association of Canada was initiated to study the implications for Canada of trade liberalization and closer economic integration among the nations bordering the North Atlantic. It is planned to issue at least twelve paperbound volumes, incorporating over twenty studies by leading Canadian and foreign economists. Despite the technical nature of much of the subject matter, the studies have been written in language designed to appeal to the non-professional reader.

The directors and staff of the Private Planning Association wish to acknowledge the financial support which made this project possible—a grant from the Ford Foundation and the contributions of members of the Association. They are also appreciative of the help that has been provided by very many individuals in the preparation and review of all the studies—in discussions and correspondence with authors, at the Association's November, 1966, conference on "Canada and the Atlantic Economy," and on other occasions.

H. E. ENGLISH
Director of Research
Atlantic Economic Studies Program

Contents

1. Economic Integration in International Capital Markets

For countries both rich and poor, proposals for policies of economic integration have stood high in popularity during the last decade. Whatever the call of interest groups and the popular prejudice for tariff protection, many a plan has been devised for groups of countries to attain integration by tearing down barriers to trade, and a surprising number have gone into effect. Everyone associates economic integration with the elimination of governmental restrictions to commodity trade among nations, and economists for many years have studied the effects of such measures.

Just as the movement of goods between countries may be either free or impeded, so may the movement of capital. Yet the voice of the people is seldom heard crying for either the freeing or the shackling of international flows of capital. Economists have likewise given little attention until recent years to the theoretical effects of capital-market integration—and less attention still to measuring these effects in real life. This study attempts to describe the prevailing degree of integration of Canada's capital markets into those of the United States. This phenomenon has, of course, occurred without there being any formal economic alignment between the two countries, but it is none the less instructive for that. The growing interdependence of economic life among Western developed nations, which is the subject of the Private Planning Association's Atlantic Economic Studies Program, probably derives more from the increasingly international spread of private market institutions than from the establishment of special intergovernmental arrangements. Thus the informal integration of capital markets in North America is as valid a subject for study in this context as is the development of customs unions and free trade areas in Western Europe.

The object of the study, then, will be to assess the implications of North American capital-market integration for the performance of the Canadian economy. The enquiry necessarily draws upon an extensive analysis of the Canadian statistical record of the last two decades, particularly the years of the fluctuating exchange rate; the details of that investigation are published elsewhere.[1] Here we summarize its results and relate them to the policy problems of Canada's immediate past and the prospects for the future.

[1]Caves and Reuber, with R. W. Baguley, J. M. Curtis, and R. Lubitz, *Capital Transfers*

1. Integration in capital markets

When looked at closely, economic integration turns out not to be a simple concept. It will help to give some attention to its general meaning before turning to the facts about the Canadian economy. We say that a commodity market is fully integrated when no artificial barriers or imperfections keep the product in question from flowing freely from any buyer to any seller within it. The economic test of an integrated market is for the same price to prevail throughout it, since we detect the force of a restriction thrown across a market by the fact that buyers caught behind the restriction have to pay a higher price for the product than that received by sellers outside it. At national boundaries, tariffs, quantitative restrictions on imports ("quotas"), or other weapons in the modern arsenal of "non-tariff barriers" to trade might preclude economic integration. Each of them, if it is effective, forces up the price behind the barrier and prevents a single price from prevailing throughout the world market. It thereby tends to distort the pattern of production and consumption in different national markets, causing too much to be produced behind the protective barrier, too little to be consumed.

Though we customarily think of government controls doing the job, private market restrictions may also block the integration of commodity markets. International cartel agreements, dividing national markets among their member producers, are a traditional example. Recent agreements among nations to promote integration, such as the Treaty of Rome establishing the European Economic Community, often contain elaborate plans to remove private as well as public impediments to integration. The treaty attacks tariffs and other public restrictions on trade as well as such private barriers as cartels and arbitrary structures of transport rates. It goes further to seek to harmonize national social legislation and social welfare taxes which, when they differ among countries, can distort patterns of production and consumption even if they do not block the creation of a single international price for a given product.[2]

and Economic Policy: Canada, 1951–1962, Harvard Economic Studies, Cambridge, Massachusetts, Harvard University Press, 1970.
[2]Definitions of integration sometimes treat as impediments to integration anything that prevents the establishment of a competitive equilibrium (or "shadow") price in the relevant international markets. It seems useful, however, to distinguish, as we have in the text, between imperfections which block the establishment of a single price in the market for a single good and imperfections which cause a price to be an inappropriate one but without precluding a single "world" price. Throughout this discussion we neglect the complication of transport costs. Prices of goods should of course differ between importing and exporting markets by the long-run marginal cost of transportation. Another complication which we neglect is the exchange rate, the link between national structures of money costs and prices, which also must satisfy equilibrium conditions.

Capital markets, like commodity markets, may be either fully or incompletely integrated, depending on whether or not public or private barriers impede the international movement of capital. Governments often restrict the flow of capital across national boundaries, just as they restrict the flow of goods. The reasons are rather different, however. A tariff is typically placed on imports of a commodity to improve the welfare of its home producers, but capital inflows are rarely blocked to favour domestic producers of capital—i.e., savers hoping for a higher interest rate. Restraints are somewhat more frequently placed on exports of capital, however, for a symmetrical reason—to keep capital at home and thus make it cheap for domestic borrowers. This control operates just like one on the export of a raw material, for the purpose of cheapening it for domestic processors. Most restrictions on capital flows, however, probably have little or nothing to do with protecting one group or another. Instead they aim at keeping the balance of payments in equilibrium.

Barriers to market integration, we saw, may be created through private efforts as well as by government action. The extent of private barriers to integrated capital markets is a more complicated business than it is for commodities. In a product market, it is not hard to tell whether or not the "law of one price" is satisfied. Nor is it for a single bond or share that is widely marketed. For "capital" in the broad sense of purchasing power over currently produced output, however, the test for market integration of a single price would require us to find equal rates of return on all classes of comparable investment opportunities—comparable in such matters as riskiness and time to maturity—and not just on financial assets. In practice it is impossible to tell how close we are to attaining this condition, since we must know not just the prices of securities but also the real rates of return on all investment projects—indeed, on potential projects as well as on those actually undertaken. We have to settle for spotting the sources of imperfection, such as capital rationing and the lack of information about distant alternatives, and try to make rough assessments.

Though the test is rough, it is not hard to decide that Canada's long-term capital market is rather closely integrated with that of the United States, and has been for some time. The degree of integration keeps improving through the development of private institutions in the capital market. Neither the Canadian nor foreign governments regularly maintain important restrictions on capital flows across the Canadian border, but these do appear occasionally. The United States' Interest Equalization Tax was designed specifically to segregate the U.S. portfolio capital market by taxing foreign issues in the American market by an amount generally sufficient to offset the advantage of lower interest rates there. Canada was excluded from this restriction on the basis of an agreement that her advantageous position would not be used to increase her official reserves of foreign exchange. The purpose of this tax, first imposed in 1963, was to plug the increasing drain on the U.S. balance of payments made by long-term foreign lending.

The remarkable degree of capital-market integration in North America springs into focus when contrasted to the recent emergence of a lesser degree of integration among other capital markets in the North Atlantic community.[3] Prior to 1958, extensive controls limited the use that holders of the major European currencies might make of them for international capital transactions. Not only were limits placed on international capital transactions in a nation's currency by its *own* citizens, but in the earlier postwar years restrictions even rested on the use made of a currency by foreigners coming into possession of it. The latter type of restriction was removed by the restoration of "external convertibility" for most countries around 1958, creating at least limited opportunities for international capital movements. Internal freedom to undertake international capital transactions remained at least somewhat restricted in many cases, however. Britain still requires that foreign security purchases be financed by foreign security sales, although Austria and Switzerland freely permit their nationals to buy foreign securities. Most European countries maintain strict controls on the issue, in their national capital markets, of foreign securities denominated in their own currencies, and estimates place the volume of transactions of this type at only a few percent of total European issues of new long-term securities.[4] They have followed (or preceded!) the United States' example in varying the severity of these restrictions in relation to their balance of payments positions.

The most important new source of closer capital-market integration in the North Atlantic community during the last decade has been the rise of the Euro-dollar market. Broadly speaking, this is a market for bank deposits in national currencies held outside the country of issue. By providing many short-term lenders or borrowers with a money market having greater breadth, convenience or safety, lower transactions costs, or fewer constraints and regulations than their national markets, it has increased the degree of integration of short-term capital markets for many countries. Its long-term adjunct, the European market for dollar-denominated bonds, has opened a new channel for collecting savings in countries with poorly organized capital markets, making capital available to borrowers in countries with

[3]For a good general account see J. S. G. Wilson, "The Internationalisation of Capital Markets," *Three Banks Review*, No. 62, June 1964, pp. 3–24.
[4]Sidney E. Rolfe, *Capital Markets in Atlantic Economic Relationships*, Boulogne-sur-Seine, The Atlantic Institute, 1967; "Recent Developments in International Capital Markets," *Federal Reserve Bank of New York Monthly Review*, XLVIII, Oct. 1966, pp. 225–9.

high interest rates and letting a lender and a borrower from two different nations denominate their respective assets or liabilities in a "vehicle currency" (usually U.S. dollars) that they feel is less risky than either of their national currencies.

The effects of the Euro-dollar market on the integration of short-term capital markets have been particularly striking.[5] The fast-widening participation of financial institutions in this market has rapidly increased the opportunities for transactions open to foreign holders or would-be holders of U.S.-dollar assets and at the same time has raised the effective competition among the financial institutions themselves. It has clearly reduced the degree to which the tightness of national money markets can get out of line from country to country, since banks in countries with tight conditions can borrow in the Euro-dollar market and either lend in dollars to domestic borrowers or swap into their own currencies to gain increased reserves. Conversely, banks or non-bank holders of funds who find themselves facing easy local credit conditions can often make loans in the Euro-dollar market for higher rates of interest. Where tight or easy credit conditions reflect the wishes of a country's central bank, these actions of course appear to frustrate official policy, and new devices have been adopted selectively to block or control this monetary integration. Banking systems have been required to balance their foreign-currency assets and liabilities (thus curtailing their ability to increase their home-currency reserves by borrowing Euro-dollars and swapping), or have incurred restrictions on foreign-currency loans to domestic borrowers.

These brief remarks about the fast-increasing degree of integration in international capital markets serve not only to underline the meaning of financial integration but also to illustrate some of its effects which will be explored in greater detail in this study. The integration of capital markets means that lenders are aware of opportunities for profitable investment (or borrowers, opportunities for bargain funds) beyond their own borders, and a situation in which returns on investment in one country lie above those elsewhere tends to bring an inflow of capital large enough to eliminate it. That is, closely integrated capital markets are typically marked by high elasticities of international capital movement in response to differences between countries in the rate of return.[6] Close integration in turn has a number of implications for economic welfare and economic policy.

[5]For recent analyses, see F. H. Klopstock, *The Euro-dollar Market: Some Unresolved Issues*, Essays in International Finance, no. 65, Princeton, International Finance Section, 1968; and A. K. Swoboda, *The Euro-dollar Market: An Interpretation*, Essays in International Finance, no. 64, Princeton, International Finance Section, 1968.
[6]This statement should not be construed to define integrated capital markets as those marked by near-infinite elasticities of capital flow. Investors might be fully aware of

First, there is some presumption that the movement of capital from a place where its rate of return is low to one where it is high leads to an increase in real income for both areas together. This follows directly if the market rate of return in the two areas corresponds to a real rate of return on capital, so that the shift reduces total output in the exporting region by less than it increases it in the importing region. This welfare gain is subject to all the qualifications customary in this sort of analysis. Just who winds up with the increased income—the lender, the borrower, the tax authorities, etc.—cannot be predicted without additional information. It is possible that some individual or group will become worse off. Thus, identifying the welfare gain requires either that we ignore changes in the distribution of income or that we suppose existing policies (tax structures, social welfare benefits, etc.) are adjusted so that the distribution remains appropriate.[7]

This welfare analysis of long-term capital flows assumes that full employment prevails, implying that countries cope successfully with the problems of stabilizing domestic employment. Another significant aspect of capital-market integration lies in its relation to countries' efforts to maintain full employment and secure a sufficiently high and stable rate of economic growth. The ease of keeping the balance of payments in equilibrium, under a fixed exchange rate, may also be affected. The more readily does capital flow across national borders in response to economic disturbances, the more likely is it to affect these policy targets. The consequence may be either to help or hinder the pursuit of these policy goals. Consider, for example, the effect of a falling unemployment rate on the balance of payments (with a fixed exchange rate). When employment is high and income growing fast, the current account of the balance of payments tends to be adverse as more imports are pulled in and exports possibly discouraged by high levels of domestic demand. At the same time, high prospective returns on investment tend to pull in foreign capital (or reduce its outflow), producing a favourable shift in the capital account of the balance of payments. Just the *right* degree

foreign profit opportunities and face no obstacles to international capital transactions, yet be reluctant to add substantial foreign assets to their portfolios without a significant yield differential. Capital-rationing and transactions costs might likewise intervene. (See S. C. Tsiang, "The Theory of Forward Exchange and the Effects of Government Intervention on the Forward Exchange Market," *IMF Staff Papers*, VII, April 1959, pp. 80–2.) Nonetheless, in practice the closer integration of international capital markets during the last decade or so has unquestionably been coupled with higher elasticities.
[7]For recent contributions to the welfare economics of international capital movements, see Marvin Frankel, "Home versus Foreign Investment: A Case Against Capital Export," *Kyklos*, XVIII, no. 3, 1965, pp. 411–32; R. W. Jones, "International Capital Movements and the Theory of Tariffs and Trade," *Quarterly Journal of Economics*, LXXXI, Feb. 1967, pp. 1–38; W. M. Corden, "Protection and Foreign Investment," *Economic Record*, XLIII, June 1967, pp. 209–32.

of integration and capital-flow sensitivity could thus preserve balance of payments equilibrium in the face of a varying growth rate, with the deficit in the current account and surplus in the capital account just offsetting each other during periods of prosperity. Too little capital response would produce a deficit in the over-all balance of payments during prosperity, and a surplus in depression; too much would generate the reverse pattern of difficulties.[8] In chapter 2 below we shall consider the extent to which disturbances in capital flows may affect the pursuit of domestic policy goals concerning growth, full employment, and payments equilibrium.

A third important effect of capital-market integration is on the leverage of domestic economic policy, or on the channels through which it works. Recall the evidence, mentioned above, that the Euro-dollar market has at times tended to frustrate the efforts of monetary authorities trying to keep credit tight within a country. When bank excess reserves are low and interest rates rising, short-term capital tends to flow in. If the exchange rate is fixed, the authorities have little choice but to buy up the extra foreign exchange poured onto the market by the capital inflow, thereby providing the banking system with the very liquidity that they are trying to dry up. Under these particular circumstances, the integration of short-term capital markets frustrates monetary policy actions undertaken for purposes of domestic stabilization. A complicated and fast-developing body of economic theory has appeared in recent years to identify the circumstances under which capital-market integration helps or hampers the exercise of domestic policy and to provide recipes for the successful management of policy when close integration exists. In chapter 3 below we outline this theory and estimate how extensively the present degree of capital-market integration affects the management of Canadian economic policy.

2. Determinants of capital flows to Canada

As background to a study of the effects of capital-market integration, we have sought to identify the determinants that economic theory would nominate for the major classes of capital inflow to Canada and to measure their

[8]Jeffrey G. Williamson's examination of the U.S. experience suggests that capital-account swings more than offset current-account movements associated with varying levels of domestic prosperity and growth. See his *American Growth and the Balance of Payments, 1820–1913*, Chapel Hill, University of North Carolina Press, 1964. Canadian experience has not been collated in quite this way, but would probably lead to the same conclusion. See G. M. Meier, "Economic Development and the Transfer Mechanism: Canada, 1895–1913," *Canadian Journal of Economics and Political Science*, XIX, Feb. 1953, pp. 1–19; Vernon W. Malach, *International Cycles and Canada's Balance of Payments, 1921–33*, Canadian Studies in Economics, No. 1, Toronto, University of Toronto Press, 1954, pp. 52–6; and Royal Commission on Banking and Finance, *Report*, Ottawa, Queen's Printer, 1964, chap. 5.

TABLE I

CONDENSED CANADIAN BALANCE OF INTERNATIONAL PAYMENTS, ANNUAL, 1946–65
($ million)

	1946	1947	1948	1949	1950	1951	1952	1953	1954	1955	1956
1. Current receipts	3,365	3,748	4,147	4,089	4,230	5,147	5,673	5,493	5,248	5,859	6,475
2. Current payments	3,002	3,699	3,696	3,912	4,549	5,659	5,486	5,941	5,672	6,546	7,847
3. Current-account balance	+363	+49	+451	+177	−319	−512	+187	−448	−424	−687	−1,372
Capital account:											
4. Direct investment, net	+26	+66	+86	+107	+260	+290	+275	+380	+335	+360	+545
5. Net new issues of securities	−312	−265	+35	−42	−74	+227	+234	+189	+128	−19	+26
6. Other long-term capital flows	−648	−511	−74	−122	+19	+96	+52	+112	+97	+106	+224
7. Total long-term flows	−934	−710	+47	−57	+205	+613	+561	+681	+560	+447	+1,295
8. Change in Canadian-dollar holdings of foreigners	+96	+7	−21	+41	+228	−196	−70	−35	+20	+80	−27
9. Trade in outstanding securities	+219	−12	−4	+28	+405	+52	−106	−32	+39	−33	+195
10. Other capital movements	−10	−3	+19	−61	+203	+98	−535	−204	−71	+149	−43
11. Total short-term flows	+305	−8	−6	+8	+836	−46	−711	−271	−12	+196	+125
12. Change in official reserves (increase —)	+266	+668	−492	−128	−722	−56	−37	+38	−124	+44	−48

TABLE I (continued)

	1957	1958	1959	1960	1961	1962	1963	1964	1965	1966[a]	1967[a]
1. Current receipts	6,529	6,452	6,813	7,136	7,788	8,423	9,289	10,747	11,481	13,341	14,945
2. Current payments	7,980	7,589	8,300	8,369	8,716	9,253	9,810	11,171	12,611	14,478	15,370
3. Current-account balance	−1,451	−1,137	−1,487	−1,233	−928	−830	−521	−424	−1,130	−1,137	−425
Capital account:											
4. Direct investment, net	+465	+390	+485	+620	+480	+400	+145	+175	+410	+690	+490
5. Net new issues of securities	+666	+530	+448	+182	+247	+410	+580	+718	+850	+961	+954
6. Other long-term capital flows	+91	+144	+75	+92	+138	−6	+21	0	−92	+31	+329
7. Total long-term flows	+1,222	+1,064	+1,008	+894	+865	+804	+746	+893	+1,168	+1,682	+1,773
8. Change in Canadian-dollar holdings of foreigners	−33	+105	+16	+123	−27	−10	+17	+12	+45	0	+23
9. Trade in outstanding securities	+98	+89	+170	+35	+65	−116	−109	−73	−304	−663	−387
10. Other capital movements	+59	−12	+281	+142	+315	+307	+13	−45	+378	−241	−966
11. Total short-term flows	+124	+182	+467	+300	+353	+181	−79	−106	+119	−904	−1,330
12. Change in official reserves (increase —)	+105	−109	+11	+39	−290	−155	−146	−363	−157	+359	−18

[a]Preliminary.
Sources: DBS, *The Canadian Balance of International Payments: A Compendium of Statistics from 1946 to 1965*, Ottawa, Queen's Printer, 1967, and Bank of Canada, *Statistical Summary: Supplement*, 1967.

strength and reliability. The following paragraphs summarize our evidence in qualitative terms.[9]

Economists customarily divide capital flows into long-term and short-term. The arbitrary boundary line is normally an elapsed time of one year between the contracting of a loan and its repayment. The short-term flows contain a number of different sorts of transactions. Typically grouped together as "changes in Canadian-dollar holdings of foreigners" are changes in foreign holdings of Canadian treasury bills and bank deposits (see line 8 of Table I, which provides a condensed version of Canada's balance of international payments for the period 1946–67). The changes in the stock of foreign holdings of Canadian currency and treasury bills are, of course, much smaller than the total turnover of them that typically takes place, as many short-term transactions are made and unwound within the year.[10] A second category of capital flows usually regarded as short-term is trade in outstanding securities. A capital inflow occurs via this channel when foreigners buy a previously issued Canadian bond or stock or when a Canadian sells a similar foreign bond or stock that he has previously purchased. Although the securities in question are typically long-term, this type of capital flow is usually thought to behave more like a short-run transfer, because the motives of the buyers and sellers are closely affected by short-run movements in the securities' prices.[11] Finally, a varied group of short-term capital movements are lumped together in Table I (and in government statistics) as "other capital movements" (line 10). This item includes changes in Canadians' bank balances abroad (i.e., holdings of foreign currency) and in foreign holdings of Canadian commercial and finance-company paper. Thus, it reflects (net) foreign financing of a portion of Canadian imports as well as borrowing for assorted domestic commercial and financial purposes. It also includes (among miscellaneous capital transactions) the residual error of estimation in the Canadian balance of payments, stemming from the statisticians' inability to detect or place correct valuations on all international transactions. Although it would be preferable

[9]For detailed information see Caves and Reuber, *Capital Transfers*, chap. 2.
[10]The following table gives the total annual turnover of Canadian treasury bills and the annual net change in the stock held abroad ($ million):

	1959	1960	1961	1962
Total turnover	369	380	375	460
Change in outstanding stock	+14	+45	+58	+4

DBS, *The Canadian Balance of International Payments*, 1960, p. 42; *ibid.*, 1961 and 1962, p. 62.
[11]Our own statistical research shows that trade in outstanding securities consistently behaves more like other types of short-term capital movements than it does like movements of newly issued long-term securities. Also see R. A. Radford, "Canada's Capital Inflow, 1946–53," *IMF Staff Papers*, IV, Feb. 1955, pp. 226–7.

to have this residual error shown separately, if it must be lumped in some-where then short-term capital movements are probably the right place. Research in the United States has shown that swings in the "errors and omissions" item in the U.S. balance relate more closely to recorded short-term capital movements than to any other measured payments flow. This is because a variety of short-term capital transactions go unrecorded either through statistical oversight or because the transactor wishes to conceal them. Probably the same pattern holds for Canada.

What forces determine the level of these short-term capital flows across the Canadian border? The key factor is clearly differences between Canada and other countries in the various short-term interest rates. Since most transactions occur with U.S. or British subjects or with foreign lenders whose alternative would be to hold U.S. or U.K. short-term securities, Canadian differentials from those countries are the most important. Several short-term interest rates may wield a significant influence—certainly those on treasury bills and prime commercial paper. These rates move rather closely together in any given country's money markets, so that international differences in treasury bill rates contribute quite a satisfactory explanation of these capital flows. We found the differentials between the Canadian treasury bill rate and the U.S. and U.K. rates to be significant regulators of short-term flows, though with the former much the more important. The elasticity of these with respect to the Canadian treasury bill rate appears to be around 8 (our estimates range from 7.4 to 8.7).[12]

Another factor that must also be taken into account is the forward exchange rate, or the price of Canadian currency for delivery at some time in the future (typically 90 days hence). Its importance lies in the fact that short-term international lenders often wish to avoid the risk of a fluctuation in the foreign exchange rate between the time when they enter into their contract and when they disentangle it. The foreign purchaser of a Canadian treasury bill will receive its face value in Canadian currency when it matures; as a U.S. citizen, he may wish to sell these Canadian funds forward, in order to know (at the time he enters into the transaction) exactly what his total profit will be in his own currency. The higher the premium, or the lower the discount on the forward Canadian dollar, the greater is his profit from the transaction. The joint influence of the international interest-rate differential and the forward premium are often bundled together and expressed as the "covered interest margin," a percentage profit on a short-term international capital transaction after covering for the exchange risk. Not all short-term

[12]These and other elasticities quoted in this chapter should be viewed as minimum estimates. Our method of estimating them contains a bias that is known to be in this direction.

inflows to Canada are covered; some lenders may prefer to take the exchange risk or to wind up holding Canadian currency.[13] Enough lenders prefer to avoid the risk, however, that their behaviour makes up a powerful force determining the forward exchange rate itself. In the last ten years or so the Canadian forward rate has come to adjust so that it usually leaves no more than 0.5 percent profit on a covered transaction, in the range of the cost of undertaking the transaction itself.[14] In 1960 a wide margin opened up for short-term covered lending by Canadians, a result of the panic on the London gold market and fears concerning the U.S. dollar; but during the furor of 1962, when the Canadian exchange rate was driven down and pegged at $0.925, the forward rate adjusted so that there was never any sustained gap permitting profitable covered transactions, even when Canadian interest rates were raised sharply to defend the new fixed exchange rate.[15]

Apart from the influence of the forward exchange rate on covered capital transactions, the spot exchange rate also affected the volume of short-term lending during the period 1950–62, when the price of the Canadian dollar was allowed to fluctuate freely. The mechanism works through the impact of a change in the spot rate on what people expect the spot rate to be in the future. Consider the decision of a U.S. investor contemplating the purchase of a Canadian security. The price of the Canadian dollar has just fallen slightly. If it stays until the security matures at its new lower level, then the investor will find, when he liquidates the security and converts back into U.S. currency, that he has earned just its nominal interest rate. If the exchange rate rises to its former value, then he will also win a dividend from exchange gains when he repatriates future interest payments and principal; on the other hand, if the drop in the Canadian dollar continues, he will suffer capital losses on future repatriations. Thus, unless investors always expect the cur-

---

[13]The DBS report on the balance of payments sometimes comments on the extent to which treasury bill transactions have been covered. E.g., *The Canadian Balance of International Payments, 1959*, p. 40.

[14]Market observers have called it "the main force determining the spread between the spot and forward rates." A. I. Roome, "Foreign Exchange," *The Canadian Banker*, LXXIII, Autumn 1966, p. 25; also Royal Commission on Banking and Finance, p. 493. Our statistical work shows that correlation between the Canada-U.S. interest differential and the difference between the forward and spot rates rose over the 1950s; it was 0.40 for 1952–6, 0.62 for 1957–mid-1961.

[15]DBS, *The Canadian Balance of International Payments*, 1960, p. 44; *idem*, 1961 and 1962, pp. 63–5. For other research on the interaction of the Canadian forward-rate and short-term capital transactions see Hans R. Stoll, "An Empirical Study of the Forward Exchange Market under Fixed and Flexible Exchange Rate Systems," *Canadian Journal of Economics*, I, Feb. 1968, pp. 55–78; and Sven W. Arndt, "International Short Term Capital Movements: A Distributed Lag Model of Speculation in Foreign Exchange," *Econometrica*, XXXVI, Jan. 1968.

rent exchange rate to continue indefinitely, changes in the rate will affect their actions—but there is no way to predict *a priori* the direction of the effect because it depends on their subjective guesses. In fact, our statistical research showed that parties making short-term capital transactions across the Canadian border acted strongly as if they expected swings in the flexible rate to be reversed.[16] Of the components of short-term flows, this pattern probably appears most strongly in trade in outstanding securities and in the speed (or tardiness) with which importers (Canadian or foreign) pay for their purchases. (A Canadian importer expecting the Canadian dollar to depreciate—the price of foreign currency to rise—will hasten payments to the foreign exporter and thus extinguish his foreign borrowing; this phenomenon is known as "leads and lags in commercial payments.")[17] As we shall see, it also affects long-term capital flows.

Long-term international capital movements are traditionally divided into two classes—direct and portfolio investment.[18] A direct investment gives the foreign purchaser control over physical assets in Canada, as when foreigners buy Canadian land or buildings, establish a firm that is a subsidiary of a foreign firm, or buy enough common shares in a Canadian enterprise to gain voting control. On the other hand, when foreigners purchase Canadian corporate or government bonds or take up isolated holdings of common shares that leave effective control of the company in Canadian hands, the resulting flow is called portfolio investment. Although these two types of long-term flow shade into one another (consider a purchase of common shares that *nearly* gives foreigners control of a Canadian firm), their broad determinants are quite different.

Portfolio flows to Canada, like short-term capital movements, depend mostly on interest-rate differences between Canada and other countries.

[16]We tested this exchange-rate sensitivity using the change in the spot rate from the previous to the current quarter. We found no significant results in testing another popular hypothesis about exchange-rate expectations: that capital flows behave as if people expected the exchange rate to return to parity ($1 Canadian equals $1 U.S.). We also found no support for the suggestion that exchange-rate responses depend on the deviation of the rate from its trend—indeed, there was little long-sustained trend during this period.

[17]For information on the practices of Canadian firms in handling their foreign-exchange assets and liabilities, see John H. Young and John F. Helliwell, "The Effects of Monetary Policy on Corporations," Royal Commission on Banking and Finance, *Appendix Volume*, Ottawa, Queen's Printer, 1964, Appendix L, chaps. 8, 11. We found the balance of merchandise trade with the United States to be a significant determinant of the volume of short-term capital inflows, but it does not significantly influence the forward premium on the Canadian dollar. This suggests a good deal of speculation (i.e., uncovered positions) in trade financing.

[18]Table I also shows a miscellaneous class consisting mostly of government loans, foreign aid, and the like.

Unlike short-term loans, they cannot readily be hedged against the risk of exchange-rate fluctuations.[19] Since most newly issued Canadian securities sold abroad are sold in the United States, one might put the matter as follows: either the borrower issues his bonds payable in U.S. currency and enjoys a lower U.S. interest rate, at the price of an exchange-rate risk, or he issues his bonds in Canadian currency, avoiding the exchange risk but paying a higher interest rate. The bulk of issues in recent years have been the former "U.S. pay" variety.[20] Several classes of Canadian borrowers have been prominent in this market. Over the whole postwar period (1946–65) 41 percent of new bonds issued have originated with Canadian corporations, 15 percent with municipalities, and 31 percent have been issued or guaranteed by the provinces. The central government, as issuer or guarantor, has been less active in the foreign market. It is clear that the size of the long-term interest-rate differential between the United States and Canada influences the choice of these borrowers on whether to go to the U.S. market. The interest rates for securities from these different issuers do not move identically, and the question arises again of the best general indicator of differential borrowing costs in the two markets. The Dominion Bureau of Statistics has suggested that U.S. borrowers may attach a higher risk to a given level of foreign government securities than to domestic governments, so that the proper comparison of international interest-rate differentials might be between a foreign central government and U.S. state and municipal governments.[21] Nonetheless, we found that the differential between Canadian and U.S. central government securities provides the best general proxy for conditions in the two markets. Our estimates of the elasticity of portfolio flows in relation to the Canadian interest rate range from 9.1 to 10.6.[22] Portfolio flows include some common and preferred stocks, and the rate of dividends paid on Canadian borrowings *minus* the rate of dividends received on Canadian lendings also wields a modest influence on the portfolio inflow.

[19]A firm of course can hedge its over-all financial position by borrowing abroad if it is an exporter expecting a stream of foreign-currency receipts. Young and Helliwell (*op. cit.*, p. 340) point out that Canadian-owned corporations are hesitant to incur a long-run exchange risk by borrowing abroad in the absence of such foreign receipts.
[20]During 1946–65, 82 percent of the sales of new issues of Canadian bonds and debentures to non-residents were payable optionally or solely in foreign currency. DBS, *The Canadian Balance of International Payments: A Compendium of Statistics from 1946 to 1965*, p. 199.
[21]DBS, *The Canadian Balance of International Payments*, 1960, p. 39.
[22]When portfolio inflows are related separately to the Canadian and the U.S. rates, rather than to their differential, the response seems larger to a given change in the U.S. rate than to the Canadian rate. This may reflect a statistical bias in the latter coefficient, or it may be that the U.S. interest rate serves as a proxy for the general level of interest rates, so that we capture an "income effect" of lower rates all around stimulating more borrowing.

Fluctuations in the exchange rate might be expected to affect long-term portfolio capital flows by the same process as short-term flows, through their impact on expectations concerning future exchange rates. Paradoxically, expectations about exchange rates might have more influence on long-term borrowing than on short. This is because, given the size of the interest-rate differential that favours borrowing abroad, it takes a larger exchange-rate change to wipe out the interest advantage on a long-term loan than it does on a short-term loan. We found, however, that portfolio borrowing abroad displayed the same order and type of sensitivity to the exchange rate during the floating-rate period as did short-term flows. The explanation may be that new issues were timed to play the swings in the exchange rate, with a U.S. pay issue brought to market when the price of the Canadian dollar seemed temporarily low. It takes, on the average, a month or two from the final decision to issue long-term securities and their delivery to the purchaser, and we found deliveries during the current quarter responsive to the previous quarter's exchange rate. This behaviour of capital flows, both long-term portfolio and short-term, with regard to the exchange rate performed the valuable function of helping to stabilize the flexible rate. A drop in the price of the Canadian dollar tended to increase the outflow of securities from Canada and thus to raise the demand for Canadian dollars. This increase in demand of course mitigated the fall in the exchange rate. This exchange-rate sensitivity of capital flows had important consequences for the effectiveness of domestic stabilization policy as well; this will be explored in chapter 3.

Capital flows may be affected by expectations about future interest rates as well as future exchange rates. One theory asserts that the term structure of interest rates—the difference between the long rate and the short—depends on what future rates are expected to be; the long rate can be viewed as an average of expected future shorts, so that, if the long rate exceeds the short, the market expects future interest rates to rise. Capital inflows are then discouraged, because the rise in interest rates will mean lower future bond prices and a capital loss for today's bond-buyers. Our statistical work confirmed this prediction for both portfolio and short-term capital flows: the greater the excess of long over short rates (other things equal), the smaller is the inflow.

Besides being related to the exchange-rate and interest-rate differentials, Canadian portfolio borrowing is also related to the total volume of capital projects which Canadian governments and corporations wish to undertake. (This volume varies with the interest rate, but of course is subject to other influences as well.) There are systematic differences between new Canadian bond issues placed on the home market and those placed in the United States—principally the smaller size of the former. As a number of large projects come to fruition, a large volume of foreign borrowing becomes almost inevitable. Conversely, generous availability of long-term funds abroad may encourage the fruition of such projects. Year-to-year variations in the size of capital inflows to Canada as well as in the mixture of types of capital instruments issued clearly reflect changes in the investment projects being undertaken in Canada.[23]

The other type of long-term capital inflow, direct investment, remains to be considered. As was explained above, direct investment is principally associated with the establishment in Canada of subsidiaries of foreign firms, or enlargement of foreign equity in those firms. As Table I shows, direct inflows to Canada, net of Canadian direct investment abroad, were frequently around a half-billion dollars annually during the major boom of the 1950s. The size and the composition of direct investment flows clearly correspond to the pattern of capital formation currently under way in Canada. Waves of heavy activity in petroleum and other natural-resource development may bring heavy inflows because of the extensive participation of foreign firms in these sectors. There may be a great deal of variation from year to year in the division of direct investment between financing new capital formation and taking over existing assets.[24] As we shall see later (chapter 2), the impact of direct investment on Canadian employment may vary substantially, depending on the relative importance of new capital formation and takeovers of existing companies.

The determinants of the rate of flow of direct investment to Canada are harder to identify in specific, statistical terms than those of portfolio or short-term inflows. For one thing, direct investment in a given year may be dominated by a few large projects,[25] so that special circumstances may play a large role. For another, the general profit prospects in the Canadian industries that attract direct investment, the proximate economic force exerting the pull on foreign capital, are hard to measure objectively from the statistical record. We found quarterly changes in direct investment in Canada to be associated with current quarterly changes in Canadian gross national product, but this proves little. It might mean that a rise in GNP causes an increase in direct investment, or it might only reflect the fact that higher

[23]See e.g., DBS, *The Canadian Balance of International Payments*, 1959, p. 6.
[24]"There is evidence that most if not all of the increased net movement to Canada in 1959 of foreign direct investment capital was related to the acquisition of existing assets rather than to new capital formation. It is interesting to note that foreign direct investment inflows rose by 19 percent in 1959 while business gross fixed-capital formation remained relatively unchanged." DBS, *The Canadian Balance of International Payments*, 1959, p. 31.
[25]The eight largest projects accounted for 42 percent of the total in 1958, 48 percent in 1959, and 59 percent in 1960. DBS, *The Canadian Balance of International Payments*, 1960, p. 32.

capital formation in Canada (for whatever reason) is associated with a larger direct-investment inflow and also raises GNP. A long-familiar interpretation of the forces governing Canada's growth rate, the "staple theory," holds that variations in the level of and prospects for Canada's natural-resource-intensive exports dominate the rhythm of long-term growth and that one effect of a period of strong exports is to pull more direct investment into the country.[26] This would suggest exports in earlier periods as a significant determinant of current direct investment inflows. Autonomous developments in the Canadian domestic economy, of course, can have the same effect, and so past movements of GNP, the extent to which industrial capacity is fully utilized, and similar variables should wield some influence. Finally, since direct investment is typically undertaken by foreign corporations with funds that they could use for investment elsewhere than in Canada, corporate liquidity and investment prospects elsewhere are also likely to influence flows to Canada.[27] Compared to short-term and portfolio investment, however, direct investment is not likely to be so responsive to short-run changes in Canadian income or to the returns to investment. Aside from important changes in tax provisions and the like, it tends to alter only slowly in response to changing growth prospects and returns to capital in Canada.

In concluding this general survey of the determinants of capital inflows to Canada, we can return to the question of the degree of integration in capital markets. The measured elasticities of the response of capital flows to changes in Canadian interest rates are quite high. Furthermore, the degree of capital-market integration has been growing over the last two decades, and this growth seems likely to continue. New types of short-term international lending are always developing to tie the Canadian capital market more and more closely into world markets.[28] A statistical test showed that the Canadian

[26]See, for example, M. H. Watkins, "A Staple Theory of Economic Growth," *Canadian Journal of Economics and Political Science*, XXIX, May 1963, pp. 141–58; George H. Borts, "A Theory of Long-run International Capital Movements," *Journal of Political Economy*, LXXII, Aug. 1964, pp. 341–59.
[27]Guy V. G. Stevens, *Fixed Investment Expenditures of Foreign Manufacturing Affiliates of U.S. Firms: Theoretical Models and Empirical Evidence*, unpublished Ph.D. dissertation, Yale University, 1967. Officer also finds evidence that U.S. and U.K. corporate liquidity influences direct investment in Canada; Lawrence H. Officer, *An Econometric Model of Canada under the Fluctuating Exchange Rate*, Harvard Economic Studies, CXXX, Cambridge, Massachusetts, Harvard University Press, 1968, pp. 74–5.
[28]For instance, in 1960 "new bank instruments came into use in Canada competing for funds with other types of medium term borrowers. A heavy volume of Canadian borrowing in the form of sales to non-residents of commercial paper also began to appear." DBS, *The Canadian Balance of International Payments*, 1960, p. 47. At about the same time Canadian banks were active in attracting deposits in U.S. dollars. See Oscar L. Altman, "Canadian Markets for U.S. Dollars," *IMF Staff Papers*, IX, Nov. 1962, pp. 297–316.

long-term interest rate followed the U.S. rate much more closely from 1957 to mid-1961 than it did from 1952 through 1956.[29] As we noted above, the covered interest margin has tended more and more in recent years to stay within the range set by transactions costs. Still, integration is not sufficiently complete that the return to capital is equated in the two countries. Canadian rates normally lie above U.S. rates by a margin which measures extra transactions costs and the risk premium that foreign financial markets demand from Canadian borrowers to cover default and exchange-rate risks (except in the case of covered transactions). This differential is not absolutely constant for any class of transactions.

The consequence of this close integration, of course, is to restrict sharply the degree to which Canadian interest rates can diverge from those in other industrial countries. It has been suggested that Canadian credit conditions can tighten or loosen in sympathy with those in other countries, even if significant interest-rate movements are not involved.[30] This linkage clearly holds important implications for the role of monetary and interest-rate policy in Canada; these will be explored below in chapter 3.

3. Capital flows and Canadian policy issues

In the balance of this chapter we wish to show how questions of the causes and effects of international capital flows have permeated questions of Canadian economic policy in recent years. We shall concentrate on the period from the mid 1950s into the early 1960s, when the performance of the Canadian economy posed a number of novel dilemmas.

Since the history of this period has been told elsewhere,[31] we mention its principal features only briefly. The deficiencies in the economy's performance are clear enough. After a boom during the early and mid 1950s, it slid off into recession in 1957, experiencing unemployment rates of 7 percent or more in 1958 and again in 1960 and early 1961. The growth of real income per person came to a halt during those years. The consumer price index continued a modest upward drift in the face of high unemployment, with the wholesale price index doing no better than holding steady; the movements of the major price indexes just about paralleled those of their U.S. counterparts, despite the fact that the United States had significantly lower unemployment and thus would have been expected to show faster price increases. As Table I (above) shows, the heavy inflow of long-term capital

[29]The respective simple correlation coefficients (quarterly data) were 0.95 and 0.64. The standard deviation of the differential between the rates fell almost in half.
[30]David W. Slater, "International Factors in Canadian Credit Conditions," *The Canadian Banker*, LXXV, Spring 1968, pp. 5–7.
[31]Paul Wonnacott, *The Canadian Dollar, 1948–1962*, Toronto, University of Toronto Press, 1965; Irving Brecher, *Capital Flows between Canada and the United States*, Montreal and Washington, Canadian-American Committee, 1965.

of 1951–54 did not abate during the subsequent period of slow growth, but instead rose from a level of between $500 and $600 million annually to a billion dollars or more. At the time of peak inflows of capital, the fluctuating price of the Canadian dollar also rose to new heights, running at a sustained premium of 4 cents and more over the U.S. dollar.

The peak capital inflows of the late 1950s involved almost every type of borrowing. Direct investment was running about $100 million a year higher than it had been in the early part of the decade. New issues of Canadian securities were at or above $700 million per year in 1956–59, yielding a substantially smaller net inflow only because the level of retirements of previously issued securities was rising steadily. Short-term inflows were also large, particularly through trade in outstanding securities and (especially 1959–61) the residual "other capital movements," which include much commercial credit and probably also unrecorded flight capital. The current-account deficit (excess of purchases over sales of goods and services) likewise rose to more than double the level it attained during the early 1950s boom.

The government initiated efforts in 1961 to work the external value of the Canadian dollar down, in order to cheapen Canadian goods and services on world markets and thereby improve the Canadian current-account balance. During the first half of 1962, these manipulative efforts were all too well rewarded, as the fall in the Canadian dollar got out of hand and forced the authorities to scramble in order to defend a new pegged value of $0.925 U.S. for the Canadian dollar. Whatever its merits as a policy manoeuvre (and many would brand the devaluation and pegging as a major blunder), this episode provides a splendid test of the response of international capital movements to unusual movements in the exchange rate. Both long- and short-run capital flows, which during the 1950s had typically responded to exchange-rate changes in a "stabilizing" fashion that tended to limit the movement of the rate, now turned tail before determined official intervention and reinforced the downward movement of the Canadian dollar. This capital flight, which fortunately was quickly reversed through the determined stabilization effort, appears to have affected mostly Canadian-owned capital, but of practically all types: increased Canadian holdings of foreign bank balances, foreign common and preferred shares, and higher Canadian direct investment abroad.[32]

The outcome of this episode, besides returning Canada to a fixed exchange

[32]DBS, *The Canadian Balance of International Payments*, 1961 and 1962, pp. 46–7, 60. "It seems clear from analyses of the data available that a major part of the movements both from Canada in the second quarter and to it in the third represented the movement of Canadian capital. The growth of Canadian private holdings of foreign currency bank balances and similar short-term funds abroad represented an outflow in the second quarter of $208 million and Canadian direct and portfolio investment abroad

rate, was to render Canadian goods relatively cheap on world markets, providing a substantial stimulus to exports and thereby domestic investment.
Between 1961 and 1964 the current-account balance improved by half a
billion dollars, and as the boom got under way (in parallel with U.S. developments), returning Canada to a low level of unemployment, gross business
fixed-capital formation rose from about 17 percent of gross national expenditure (in 1963) to 21 percent (1966). Foreign borrowing naturally increased to finance this investment boom, and total issues of new securities
abroad exceeded one billion dollars in both 1964 and 1965. Direct investment did not show a parallel expansion.

   Throughout the late 1950s a pervasive concern was expressed over the
size of the Canadian current-account deficit and the process of financing
it through foreign borrowing. The more flamboyant charges proclaimed that
the excess of foreign purchases over foreign sales indicated that Canadians
were "living beyond their means" and having to borrow to finance their
wastrel ways. More conservatively, the DBS publications on the balance of
payments regularly expressed concern over the fact that current-account
deficits were being financed in part through short-term borrowing abroad
rather than fully through long-run borrowing.

   To clear the air on one point at the start, in any given year a current-
account deficit must be financed—after the event—by some form of capital
inflow. This follows from the method of constructing balance of payments
statistics, whereby the various net balances struck in the accounts must sum
algebraically to zero. Taking the balances as they are set forth in Table I,
this means that in any given year the current-account deficit (line 3) must
be exactly financed by the total of net long-term borrowing, public and
private (line 7), short-term private borrowing (line 11), and the reduction
in official reserves, which amounts to short-term government borrowing
(line 12).[33] If the current account is in deficit, any two of these capital
balances may show net lending, and the remaining capital balance must
still offset the total. Suppose we take the total of all Canadian current-account
deficits for the period 1950–65.[34] Total net long-term borrowing over the
same period offset 99.6 percent of that total, and net short-term private
borrowing, 16.0 percent. The total exceeds 100 percent because Canada
accumulated foreign reserves during this period and by that process made
foreign loans equivalent to 15.5 percent of the cumulative current-account

---

added a further $65 million to outflows. These items alone were as large as the net
outflow of all types of capital" (p. 47).

[33]It is too seldom understood that an increase in Canadian official reserves amounts to
foreign lending, just as much as when Canadian corporations or individuals accumulate
foreign currency. See Fritz Machlup, *Involuntary Foreign Lending.*

[34]The earlier years are clouded by the effects of postwar recovery on the balance of
payments; 1950 begins the period of sustained capital inflows.

deficit.[35] It is not clear exactly what can be concluded from these percentages, but in any case they hardly support a charge that import surpluses have been excessively financed by short-term borrowing. The questions that lurk behind this outcome, of course, are whether the current-account deficit is indeed the cause and the capital inflow the effect, and—whichever way the causal relations run—how readily one component of the Canadian balance of payments adapts to changes in another. Much popular discussion in Canada has suggested that Canadians collectively decide how much excess imports to purchase and then scratch around for a means to pay for them: i.e., that swings in the current account cause adaptive swings in the capital account. Hypothetically, the process could run just the opposite way: foreigners decide to lend to Canada, then Canadians expend the resulting purchasing power on goods and services, including imports, and thereby "requite" the financial transfer.[36] Between these possibilities lies a third explanation—given much credence by the Royal Commission on Banking and Finance for the period 1953–60[37]—that both capital inflows and current-account deficits arise from the common cause of Canadian prosperity. If the capital and trade accounts responded in just the same degree to variations in Canadian prosperity, the nation would be blessed with a most convenient mechanism for stabilizing the balance of payments. If this neat synchronization fails or if disturbances arise in either the capital or the current account, then it becomes important to know how readily one adjusts to the other. This brings us to another group of policy issues that were urgently debated in the late 1950s.

During those years, as our previous review indicated, the Canadian economy experienced high unemployment, a substantial current-account deficit, and large capital inflows. It is a standard proposition of modern income theory that a deterioration of a nation's current account, other things held constant, tends to reduce its level of employment, and an improvement tends to increase employment.[38] The idea then became firmly established in Canadian policy discussions that the deficit was somehow causing the high unemployment level, or at least that some action to reduce the deficit was a necessary side-condition for restoring full employment.[39] As Professor Barber put it, "diversion of even half of [the current-account

[35]These percentages fail exactly to cancel because of rounding errors.
[36]The classic "transfer problem" in international economic theory deals with exactly this series of adjustments following a disturbance in the capital account.
[37]*Report*, pp. 483–4.
[38]It does *not* follow that a deficit continuing at a constant level directly causes further shrinkage of income flows, although the monetary process of financing the deficit may have this effect.
[39]David W. Slater, *Canada's Balance of International Payments—When Is a Deficit a Problem?*, Montreal, Canadian Trade Committee, 1964, pp. 27–39, provides an excellent analysis of the relation between current-account deficits and unemployment policy.

deficit], either directly or indirectly, from foreign goods to Canadian output should have been sufficient ... to reduce unemployment in Canada to well below the 4 percent level."[40] The chief deficiency in the ensuing discussion, in our eyes, was its neglect of the relation of the current-account deficit to the large capital inflow, and of the inflow to Canadian monetary policy.

What does a capital inflow do to the Canadian economy? There is no doubt, we shall argue, that it tends to produce a current-account deficit. Whether or not it also tends to produce unemployment, however, is a different question. When Canada had a fluctuating exchange rate, a capital inflow unleashed two effects. First, the inflow itself constituted an increased demand for the Canadian dollar, tending to drive up its price on world currency markets. As the price rose, Canadian goods and services became more expensive to foreigners, foreign goods cheaper to Canadians, and the balance on current account tended to worsen. The other effect depended on the extent of new capital formation in Canada associated with the capital inflow. This extra investment tended to raise Canadian income and employment (through the familiar multiplier process). The higher income level in turn raised Canadian imports (and perhaps discouraged exports). It is possible that this boost to domestic income might, on its own, generate a current-account deficit big enough to offset the capital-account surplus stemming from the original capital inflow; in that case, no sustained rise in the exchange rate would have to occur, and the deterioration of the current account would not be associated with any reduction in domestic employment.[41] On the other hand, if the foreign borrowing failed to be accompanied by additional domestic capital formation, then the capital inflow tended clearly to be deflationary. Obviously everything hangs on the factual question of whether or not various types of capital inflows, arriving in Canada under varying domestic economic conditions, generate corresponding increases in capital formation. Our evidence on this is presented below in chapter 2.

Some have suggested that capital imports make a valuable contribution to the Canadian economy when full employment already prevails, because they finance an inflow of real goods and services from abroad that could not be produced at home. "In a recession or depression," however, "total demand for our goods and services falls short of our productive potential. We have a deflationary gap. We are saving enough to provide the real

[40]Clarence L. Barber, "Canada's Unemployment Problem," *Canadian Journal of Economics and Political Science*, XXVIII, Feb. 1962, p. 89.
[41]For theoretical accounts of this mechanism, see R. G. Penner, "The Inflow of Long-term Capital and the Canadian Business Cycle, 1950–1960," *Canadian Journal of Economics and Political Science*, XXVIII, Nov. 1962, pp. 527–42; and James R. Melvin, "Capital Flows and Employment under Flexible Exchange Rates," *Canadian Journal of Economics*, I, May 1968, pp. 318–33.

resources for all our investments, and we need not try to acquire real resources by borrowing abroad."[42] The weak link in this argument is its assumption that the level of investment is fixed independent of the capital inflow and that the only question is whether it shall be financed at home or abroad. If this assumption holds true, then blocking capital inflows at times of unemployment would raise aggregate demand without incurring any direct real cost. But if it is false—if extra capital inflows may be associated with extra investment, even in times of unemployment—then such a policy would be fruitless or worse. Again, the importance of measuring the linkages between capital inflow and investment expenditure is shown.

Whatever the evidence reveals about their employment effects, one wonders what caused the continued wave of capital imports in the late 1950s, after the period of rapid domestic growth had passed. A minor portion of the answer lies in the fact that Canadian domestic booms pull in long-term capital, especially direct investment, with something of a lag. In the first year of a domestic boom, the current account deteriorates, but long-term capital inflows do not immediately rise to fill the gap; a large short-term inflow occurs, as in 1955 and 1965.[43] At the other end, long-term inflows may tend to persist after the boom inducing them has receded. This pattern might explain some of the heavy inflows in the late 1950s. The major explanation, however, lies in a failure of Canadian economic policy that is now well documented[44]—restrictive monetary and debt-management policy which kept Canadian interest rates high (in the face of sustained unemployment) and attracted a large inflow of portfolio capital. This situation resulted from spectacularly poor coordination of Canada's major domestic policy instruments, in which substantial government deficits, the natural passive consequence of domestic unemployment, were combined with a tightly reined growth of the money supply and a massive effort (in 1958) to increase the term to maturity of the government debt in the hands of the public. Under some circumstances it may be proper to play off the instruments of policy one against the other in this fashion, but those circumstances were not present for Canada. The reactions of international capital flows were hostile to the achievement of the nation's domestic objectives.

As we noted above, both short-term capital inflows and long-term portfolio borrowing are highly sensitive to the differential between Canadian

[42]Ian M. Drummond, *The Canadian Economy: Organization and Development*, Homewood, Illinois, Richard D. Irwin, 1966, pp. 80–1.
[43]DBS, *The Canadian Balance of International Payments*, 1963, 1964, and 1965, p. 11. Our statistical work uncovered a systematic alternation between short-term and portfolio (but not direct) investment.
[44]E.g., Barber, "Canada's Unemployment Problem"; Wonnacott, *The Canadian Dollar*, pp. 215–53.

and foreign (principally U.S.) interest rates. The lengthening of the government debt drove down long-term bond prices as more of these securities were
unloaded on the public. The elevation of long-term interest rates by this
policy was augmented by tight money, which dampened demand in the
bond market. The resulting outflow of securities to the United States led
to a high level of demand for the Canadian dollar, pushing its price to the
peak levels observed during these years. In the face of high interest rates,
the increased capital inflow could not be expected to stimulate heavy investment spending in Canada. At the same time, the high exchange rate spurred
deterioration of the current account and added to the deflationary forces.
Finally, the "easy" fiscal policy stemming from the government deficit could
not help much to relieve unemployment, because the financial counterpart
of the budget deficit was increased sales of securities, and these only rein-
forced the trend to high interest rates and low bond prices. Qualitatively,
the reverse combination of policies—tight fiscal and easy money—might
have served Canada well indeed. Low interest rates would have discouraged
the capital inflow and lowered the external value of the Canadian dollar,
improving the trade balance and avoiding the accumulation of foreign debt
that was needless under the circumstances, in that it was induced under
conditions in which it probably contributed only modestly to increasing
the domestic capital stock. Instead, the highly unsatisfactory combination of
policies eventually led the government to undertake a direct attack on the
external value of the Canadian dollar beginning in late 1960, and the government thereby blundered into an excessive devaluation and needless pegging
in 1962.[45]

This diagnosis, now widely accepted among Canadian economists, contains not only a qualitative argument about the direction of effects of economic policy, but also some implied quantitative judgments about their
speeds and sizes. How much capital do high interest rates attract? How
much do the induced capital inflows raise the price of the Canadian dollar,
and what about the discouragement to capital inflows which that elevated
exchange rate provides? How much does the current account deteriorate
following a given rise in the exchange rate, and how quick is its response?
In chapter 3 below we attempt quantitative answers to these questions.

If a small increase in the spread of interest rates between Canada and
the United States would produce an unlimited inflow of capital, then clearly
Canadian policy would be powerless to change the interest rate. That Cana-

[45]Some foreign economists have found in this episode support for a case against the
flexible exchange rate. A more reasonable conclusion would be that the flexible
exchange rate cannot protect a country against wrongly conceived policies and that, in
conjunction with interest-elastic capital flows, it may amplify the evil consequences of
some types of error.

dian interest rates are at least somewhat locked in to foreign levels has been noted in policy discussions, leading to concern about the domestic effectiveness of monetary policy. This impact of capital-market integration was illustrated again in 1967 in the marked parallel rise of interest rates (especially short-term) in Canada and the United States.[46] U.S. credit conditions were eased in late 1966, but from spring 1967 to the end of the year interest rates rose to record levels. Canadian rates moved in the same general pattern. The Canadian treasury bill rate, however, outran the U.S. rate from the spring through July, rose more slowly August through October, then faster through early 1968. The Canadian movement was out of phase because a strong Canadian balance of payments position at the end of the second quarter, owing to heavy inflows of portfolio and direct investment, induced some easing of short-term credit and (apparently) action to lower the forward price of the Canadian dollar. A large short-term capital outflow followed; coupled with a worsening in other payments categories later in the year and the shudders of the international monetary system which began in November, it forced a renewed tightening. Canadian policy was able to modify the timing of the over-all increase but apparently could not have averted it.

Did this lack of freedom to vary interest rates mean that Canadian monetary policy was without power in 1967 to control domestic aggregate demand? One's instinct would be to answer yes, and that answer would be substantially correct—*but only because the exchange rate is now fixed.* The extent to which capital-market integration denies Canada the freedom to vary interest rates is another factual question to be treated below. But the significance of this lock-in can be learned only by relating it to a theoretical model that tracks down all the effects of a monetary-policy change, including exchange-rate and balance of payments adjustments.[47] In the late 1950s the monetary authorities may have enjoyed little more freedom to vary interest rates than they do now, but they could still wield an influence over domestic demand and employment. Alas, this influence was misdirected at just the time when it would have been most valuable.

The next two chapters explore in detail the economic theory that underlies these deductions and the results of our statistical investigations of the important economic relations which they describe. Chapter 2 is concerned with the extent to which capital flows have constituted an independent disturbance to the Canadian economy and with the process of adjustment to

[46]This episode is reviewed by Slater, "International Factors in Canadian Credit Conditions," pp. 9–12.
[47]Cf. R. A. Mundell, "Capital Mobility and Stabilization Policy under Fixed and Flexible Exchange Rates," *Canadian Journal of Economics and Political Science,* XXIX, Nov. 1963, pp. 475–85.

disturbances from this quarter. That is, it asks the following questions. When capital inflows varied, was it due to Canadian forces or to outside changes? When capital-flow disturbances occur, how does the Canadian economy adjust to them?

Chapter 3 deals with the management of domestic policy in a world of mobile capital. It indicates how the leverage and the timing of the effects of fiscal, monetary, and debt management is altered by these capital movements.

2. Adjustment to Disturbances in Canada's Capital Inflows

Most people would accept the view that living in an open economy, whatever its benefits, imposes the cost of adjusting to disturbances in trade and payments that emanate from the seething outside world. This popular view is not necessarily a very accurate or fruitful one. For one thing, as Harry Johnson has pointed out, it implies the questionable assumption that, while foreigners might readily act in a way to upset the domestic applecart, the natives would never do so. For another, under some conditions adjustment may come more easily to a more integrated (open) economy than to a less integrated (closed) one.[1] Nonetheless, the attitude does raise two eminently reasonable questions about capital-flow disturbances and the Canadian economy. First, to what extent have outside disturbances in international capital flows forced adjustment processes on the Canadian economy? Second, what forms do these adjustments take, and how troublesome do they prove?

1. Disturbances from capital inflows

The extent to which capital inflows have transmitted disturbances to the Canadian economy is one of those questions which seem simple at first glance but prove quite complicated on close analysis. As we pointed out in chapter 1, capital inflows are closely related to features of the Canadian economy—interest rates, the exchange rate, and the like. Our statistical evidence tells us that a substantial portion of the swings in capital inflows is due to changes in these Canadian magnitudes. There is little point in calling capital-flow variation from these sources an outside disturbance to Canada, even though it may impose an adjustment burden. We can, of course, discover what portion of the variation in capital flows is *not* explained by the various plausible domestic factors, and attribute that to external disturbances. (Note that statistical methods will tell what portion of the fluctuations of capital flows around their average levels is due to foreign

[1]E.g., R. I. McKinnon and W. E. Oates, *The Implications of International Economic Integration for Monetary, Fiscal, and Exchange Rate Policy*, Princeton Studies in International Finance, No. 16, Princeton, International Finance Section, Princeton University, 1966, pp. 10–12.

forces, but not what portion of the total inflow.) We shall use that technique below, although by itself it is not necessarily very informative. If we conclude that 60 percent of the swings in a category of capital flows are due to domestic factors, and 40 percent to foreign ones, so what?

To deal with this problem of comparative evaluation, we employ two techniques. One is simple and can be explained directly. The other requires rather elaborate calculations and will emerge later in this chapter. The first method harks back to some policy questions mentioned above that have often been raised in Canada: do Canadians borrow abroad to finance current-account deficits, or have the current-account deficits been caused by the foreign borrowing? To take a third possibility, have swings in the current- and capital-account balances both resulted from domestic disturbances, such as swings in the rate of unemployment? If cause and effect took place at the same time, we would have no chance of sorting out which is which. However, these causal links, any of which is logically plausible, would take time to operate—enough time that we should spot variations in a series that embodies primarily "cause" occurring before variations in another that registers primarily "effect."

Using several different statistical techniques to implement this method, we tested for predominant causal relations among the major components of the balance of payments.[2] Over the period 1951–62 there is no question but that changes in the Canadian balance of trade preceded changes in the net inflow of long-term capital.[3] Our evidence is not completely definite on the length of the lag, but it appears that, at the most, swings in the long-term capital balance follow the trade balance after four quarters; and at the least, they coincide with it. Comparing movements of the long-term capital balance with the total current-account balance (services as well as trade), there is somewhat more of a tendency for swings to coincide, rather than for capital to lag, though it remains clear that capital lags rather than leads. The explanation for this difference is probably that the current account includes international net payments of interest and dividends. If some capital flows coincide with trade-balance swings and (characteristically) start yielding interest and dividend payments one to three quarters later, swings in the current-account balance might appear to lag nearly a year after swings in the trade balance.

This pattern is consistent with two popular explanations of Canadian payments patterns, but not with a third. It could reflect "export-led growth," the famous sequence described in the staple theory of Canadian growth

[2]For a full description, see Caves and Reuber, *Capital Transfers*, chap. 6.
[3]Direct, portfolio, and other long-term capital, including Canadian foreign aid, government loans, etc. (line 7 of Table I).

whereby swings in export sales and profits determine the rate of capital formation and growth of total GNP and also govern the rate of inflow of foreign capital. It is also consistent with disturbances occurring primarily in investment prospects for the domestic market. The resulting swings in domestic income and employment affect imports (and thus the current account) immediately, but their impact on capital inflows is spread over a longer time period. Finally, the pattern is *not* consistent with capital flows serving as the predominant source of disturbances to the Canadian balance of payments.

We can check these conclusions by comparing the timing of swings in the trade balance (or current account) and total short-term capital inflows. Here the results are more than a little puzzling, since short-term capital movements seem to *precede* swings in the trade and current-account balances (and long-term capital as well) by as much as a year (four quarters).[4] This relation may be a fluke, with the true pattern being the highly plausible one of short-term capital movements coinciding with changes in the current account, both because of the requirements of trade financing and because both commodity and short-term capital movements respond to short-run fluctuations in GNP. If there is an economic interpretation of the apparent lead of short capital flows, however, it may be that they respond to domestic disturbances even more quickly than does commodity trade. Taking the two payments patterns confirmed in the preceding paragraph, this would tend to suggest that domestic disturbances, rather than disturbances in the commodity export sector, dominate movements in Canada's international variables. But we cannot eliminate the explanation, though it seems an unlikely one, that autonomous movements in international short-term capital flows cause adjustments in other balance of payments variables more typically than they themselves are caused to adjust.

One way to solve the puzzle of whether current-account disturbances primarily affect income, or the other way around, is to check the lead-lag patterns of GNP in relation to the balance of payments components. The results are helpful if not decisive. Fluctuations in the current-account balance seem both to lead GNP by two to three quarters and to lag by one to two quarters. There is no significant difference between the strength of these two linkages. Short-term capital markets, however, retain the same long lead over GNP that they show over the trade balance. This evidence suggests that

---

[4]This finding should not reflect merely seasonal patterns in the data. Our statistical methods included some that made seasonal adjustments to the data and some that did not, but this conclusion emerged with equal strength in all cases. Even if our methods have failed to take sufficient account of the influence of seasonality, the results would be biased towards findings of no lags or lags in multiples of four quarters, but there should be no conversion of a true leading relation into an apparent lag, or vice versa.

export-led and domestic disturbances are both important, relative to disturbances originating in long-term capital flows; but the role of short-term capital flows remains something of a mystery.

Faced with these puzzles in the behaviour of the aggregate capital flows, we disaggregated them into their chief components. Separating direct investment out of long-term capital flows, we found that it shows some tendency to lead changes in the trade and current-account balances (and also GNP) by two quarters, although the relation between the trade balance and direct investment two quarters later remains fairly strong. Portfolio investment, however, lags unambiguously behind changes in the trade balance. These results accord closely with what we would expect theoretically; direct investment responds to general profit prospects not necessarily registered in any measures of current domestic economic activity, and thus it is likely to seem exogenous. When we disaggregate short-term capital inflows by breaking out trade in outstanding securities, it turns out to lead the trade balance and current account by one quarter, or perhaps to coincide. Other short-term capital (unfortunately, no other economically significant components can be broken out of this aggregate on a quarterly basis over the whole period) continues to show a long lead over swings in the current account.

As a further check on these lead-lag relations, we manipulated several of the major capital-flow series to remove the portion of their variation directly associated with Canadian domestic changes.[5] Lead-lag patterns were then checked between the residual variation in these capital series, which should reflect to a large degree disturbances originating outside Canada, and the other balance of payments components. In the case of direct investment, the two-quarter lead over shifts in the trade balance now appears even more distinctly, and the secondary pattern of a two-quarter lag of direct investment behind the trade balance disappears. The exogenous component of portfolio capital inflows now shows a one-quarter lead over the current-account balance. Since the balance of payments measure of net new issues of securities represents deliveries, which occur a month or two after issues are contracted for, the actual decisions affecting the portfolio inflow lead changes in the current account by between one and two quarters. Finally, the extent to which trade in outstanding securities leads the current-account balance is stretched out from one quarter to two by removing the portion induced by Canadian developments (although a fairly strong lagging component still remains).

[5]Long-term interest rates, in the case of direct investment; long-term interest rates, the unemployment rate, and net new issues of securities, in the case of net portfolio capital inflows; and long- and short-term interest differentials, in the case of trade in outstanding securities.

We mention, in passing, a test which is technically similar to those just described, although it deals with a different question: lead-lag relations between the exchange rate and major balance of payments components. Most economists, without having studied the institutional peculiarities of the Canadian fluctuating exchange rate, would probably expect the current-account balance to lag somewhat after exchange-rate swings, but for movements of the rate to coincide with the capital accounts. They would predict this because they expect that current-account flows are affected by the exchange rate, whereas swings in capital flows should affect the exchange rate (simultaneously) but not necessarily be affected by it. On the other hand, we suggested in chapter 1 that Canadian capital flows were indeed sensitive to the exchange rate in the short run, in a way that tended to combat or stave off changes in the rate. On this basis we would predict swings in the exchange rate to lag a quarter or two behind capital-account swings, but no significant relation between capital flows and the value of the exchange rate in significantly earlier periods. This pattern is exactly confirmed for both long- and short-term flows. In the case of trade flows, which might take some time to respond to the exchange rate, we might expect a significant relation with one sign for leading values of the rate (as the rate affects trade flows), one with the opposite sign for subsequent exchange-rate changes (as trade disturbances affect the rate). Only the latter pattern is evident from the data.

To summarize the evidence developed so far, disturbances intruding on the Canadian economy through international capital flows failed to dominate the balance of payments during the 1951–62 period. Instead, the pattern is largely consistent with the variations in commodity exports and domestic expenditure providing the principal sources of disturbance, to which other things adjusted. When domestic influences on the different types of capital flows are removed, then their residual variations display somewhat more clearly the role of outside disturbance—particularly direct investment and net trade in outstanding securities.

2. Effects of changes in capital flows

The importance of disturbances to the Canadian economy coming from capital inflows depends, of course, on how much trouble it is to adjust to them. The amount of "trouble" in turn depends on whether or not the changes that will occur, as the Canadian economy responds to the impact of a capital-flow disturbance, violate domestic policy goals concerning the level or stability of economic activity. With the Canadian exchange rate fixed, a key specific question of this type is the net impact of capital disturbances on the balance of payments, after all market adjustments have worked themselves out.

A. THE THEORY OF CAPITAL TRANSFERS

In chapter 1 we briefly outlined the consequences of an increased capital inflow.[6] First, income and expenditure are altered as the capital flow causes (or permits) an increase in domestic spending on capital formation by corporations or governmental units, or possibly allows households to increase their level of consumption. This rise in autonomous domestic spending probably induces some further increases in domestic expenditure (unless unemployment is quite low). Some of the extra expenditure goes for domestic goods, some for imports, and this expansion of imports (and possibly discouragement of exports through easier selling conditions in the home market) worsens the current account of the balance of payments. Note that the opposite sequence may be occurring in the lending country—less autonomous domestic spending, which eventually causes some cut in purchases of Canadian exports. It may work out that the sum of effects on the current account —due to both foreign and domestic income adjustments—just equals the size of the initial capital disturbance. In this case two important conclusions can be drawn: (1) the Canadian balance of payments is left undisturbed, since the extra capital inflow improves the capital account by the same amount that the current account worsens; (2) Canadians wind up with extra goods and services just equal in value to the amount of funds that they borrowed abroad, because they are importing that much more from abroad (or possibly retaining more home-produced goods rather than selling them as exports). We say that the financial transfer has been just "requited." How well are domestic policy goals served in this case? The balance of payments is undisturbed. Aggregate domestic expenditure cannot have fallen (because extra spending associated with the capital transfer can be no more than offset by the deterioration of the current account), and it may have increased.[7] The economy enjoys a larger real intake of goods and services (presumably for capital formation of some sort) and incurs an obligation to pay interest and, eventually, to repay principal abroad.[8]

Unfortunately, there is no reason why the income and expenditure changes associated with a capital flow should exactly requite it in this way—no more,

[6]See pp. 6, 7, and 22ff.
[7]The analysis of this paragraph draws upon extensive writings dealing with the theory of international capital transfers. For important recent contributions see Paul A. Samuelson, "The Transfer Problem and Transport Costs," *Economic Journal*, LXII, June 1952, pp. 278–304; *ibid.*, LXIV June 1954, pp. 264–89; and Harry G. Johnson, "The Transfer Problem and Exchange Stability," *Journal of Political Economy*, LXIV, June 1956, pp. 212–25.
[8]As we indicated in chapter 1, we do not deal in this study with measures of the real benefits and costs of foreign investment, nor therefore with any policy objectives concerned with them.

no less. They might produce too small a change in the current account, "underrequiting" the transfer and leaving a balance of payments surplus. Or they might produce too large a change in trade, "overrequite" the transfer and leave a deficit. When the exchange rate was flexible, an underrequited transfer caused an appreciation of the Canadian dollar on world currency markets. There was no question about shifting the current account by a sufficient amount, since the appreciation simply went on until that occurred. The end result could be deflationary, however, since the exchange-rate appreciation is itself deflationary and might more than offset any increased expenditure directly associated with the transfer. Conversely, with a flexible exchange rate, an overrequited transfer leads to depreciation of a flexible exchange rate and definitely increases real expenditure at home.

In short, economic theory tells us that capital-flow disturbances may have one set of consequences or another set. But for a factual prediction about which set is the more likely, theory will not suffice. We need to collect the facts.

B. CAPITAL FLOWS AND DOMESTIC EXPENDITURE

Of the relations among income flows in the domestic economy that play a part in responding to capital disturbances, a great deal is already known. These are the connections which policy-makers and short-term forecasters study as part of their daily business. One connection, however—that between capital flows and the various categories of domestic expenditure—has received little study, and we had to devote considerable attention to it.

Direct investment. Take first the influence of direct investment, which is simpler in principle than other types of capital inflow. Decisions to transfer purchasing power to Canada as direct investment are often, although not always, linked administratively to decisions to undertake capital spending in Canada. A U.S. corporation transfers capital to Canada in order to build and equip a Canadian subsidiary and endow it with working capital. In this case a dollar's worth of direct investment corresponds to a dollar of capital formation in Canada. Indeed, when would this not be the case? Critics of direct investment have pointed to two instances in which an amount of capital formation smaller than the inflow might result. First, the direct investment might serve to buy out an existing Canadian enterprise rather than build a new factory. The former Canadian owners might still use the proceeds for some other investment project, but the chances are good that they might not spend the whole sum, or might not spend it immediately. Second, capital formation in foreign subsidiaries, financed by direct investment, might frighten off domestic Canadian entrepreneurs, causing them to spend less than they would in the absence of aggressive foreign entrepreneurs.[9] On the other hand, two other general arguments suggest that a dollar of direct investment might be associated with more than a dollar of capital formation in Canada. Where the direct investment funds are transferred to an existing subsidiary of a foreign enterprise, they may be used in conjunction with retained earnings from the firm's past operations and thus finance a larger quantity of capital formation. Also, capital formation in industries where direct investment is common—manufacturing and natural-resource extraction—may frequently stimulate secondary investment in other industries, such as business service and public-utility enterprises.[10] An appeal to the facts is necessary.

We explored this relation by measuring the amount of extra capital formation in Canada associated with an extra dollar of direct investment, after the major Canadian domestic determinants of capital formation have been taken into account. Following other investigators, we allowed principally for two of these domestic determinants: the volume of corporate liquid assets in the form of depreciation allowances and retained earnings, and the extent to which existing Canadian manufacturing capacity is fully utilized. It seems reasonable and conservative to argue that, after the influence of these factors on capital formation is removed, any increases in capital formation that are associated with direct investment should be chalked up as the consequence of direct investment.[11]

Applying this method to data for 1951–62, we conclude that a dollar of direct investment was typically associated with more than a dollar of Canadian capital formation, generally between $1.50 and $3.00. The capital formation does not coincide with the direct investment, but rather is spread more or less evenly over the three succeeding quarters. We detected some factors which determine whether the associated capital formation falls at the high or the low end of this range. It tends to the high end when unemployment is low in Canada, towards the low end when it is high (so that less complementary investment is stimulated). It tends to be low when the volume of takeovers of Canadian companies is high. Finally, it tends to be high when foreign investment is directed towards Canadian secondary manufacturing, but low when it is directed to petroleum and mining. The

[9]A recent exponent of this view is Stephen Hymer, "Direct Foreign Investment and the National Economic Interest," *Nationalism in Canada*, ed. Peter Russell, Toronto, McGraw-Hill, 1966, pp. 191–202.

[10]Penner, "The Inflow of Long-term Capital and the Canadian Business Cycle," discusses these possibilities.

[11]For a detailed explanation of this method and the statistical results, see Caves and Reuber, *Capital Transfers*, chap. 4, which is drawn from a Ph.D. dissertation by Raymond Lubitz.

reason for this difference is that foreign subsidiaries have long been entrenched in secondary manufacturing and so can match new equity funds from abroad with retained earnings of their own to finance new projects. Direct investment in the extractive industries, on the other hand, usually goes into new ventures which secure no matching funds from other sources. Table II summarizes our estimate of the effect of direct investment on capital formation.

Portfolio investment. Extra inflows of portfolio capital are also likely to encourage additional capital formation in Canada. We cannot, however, view all decisions to borrow abroad and decisions to invest as administratively linked, as we did with direct investment. The reason for this is the ready availability of alternatives. A Canadian firm or government agency that borrows abroad could almost always borrow instead, at *some* price, in the Canadian capital market. The effect of extra supplies of foreign portfolio capital must be viewed as influencing the interest rate, or price, at which Canadians can borrow, and as having its impact on capital formation through the extra capital formation that is stimulated by cheaper funds.

To implement this approach, we first had to work out the effect of a dollar inflow of portfolio capital on the Canadian long-term interest rate. This is somewhat complicated statistically, because the Canadian interest rate also influences the size of the portfolio capital inflow (as we explained in chapter 1). An autonomous one-dollar increase in portfolio investment in Canada actually produces a total increase in the portfolio inflow of somewhat less than one dollar, because it depresses the Canadian interest rate and discourages other would-be investors in Canada. We used various statistical methods to allow for this interdependence, concluding that it probably takes an extra $39 million of portfolio inflow to drive the Canadian long-term interest rate down one-tenth of one percent (i.e., ten basis points). As an absolute maximum, it might take as much as $132 million.[12] Under one set of circumstances, the needed portfolio inflow to drive down the Canadian long rate by this amount might even be as little as $13 million. This would be if the extra capital flows into Canada because of a fall in the U.S. long-term interest rate. A fall in a long-term interest rate is, of course, the same thing as a rise in the prices of outstanding bonds. We found that American bond prices wield a strong influence on the prices expected to prevail in Canadian bond markets and that those expectations themselves tend strongly to shift Canadian bond prices without much actual change in capital flows taking place.

We now have a range of estimates of the size of a disturbance in portfolio

[12]These methods and results are explained in detail in Caves and Reuber, *Capital Transfers*, chap. 3, drawn from a Ph.D. dissertation by Robert W. Baguley.

capital inflows necessary to drive down Canadian long-term interest rates by one-tenth of a percent. The increase in Canadian capital formation that would result from this cheapening of funds depends on the interest-elasticity of investment. For this we drew estimates from two recent studies. Thomas A. Wilson has calculated an interest-sensitivity of business capital formation suggesting that a fall of one percent in the cost of capital causes an increase of two-thirds of a percent in business capital formation. This increase is spread over about a two-year period, with the peak in the induced capital spending coming in the fourth quarter after the fall in interest rates.[13] Similarly, Lawrence B. Smith has estimated the effect of a fall in the cost of capital on the level of residential construction.[14] Although we shall use his figure, it is not really a demand response to price. Rather, it reflects the increase in funds available for residential construction that used to occur when market long-term interest rates fell relative to the former ceiling interest rate for mortgages guaranteed under the National Housing Act. Table II shows both the extra capital formation that would result from a one-tenth of a percent fall in Canadian long-term interest rates and the range of increases in portfolio capital inflows that might be needed to cause this drop.

Short-term capital inflows. The effect of disturbances in inflows of short-term capital can be viewed in the same way as the effect of disturbances in portfolio inflows. They tend to drive down the Canadian interest rate—in this case, the short-term rate—and to increase domestic expenditure to the extent that it is sensitive to the short-term rate.

Again, we face a complicated statistical problem in measuring these effects, because increased capital inflows drive down Canadian interest rates, but lower interest rates also tend to shrink the inflow. This interdependence has to be taken into account. Furthermore, as we noted in chapter 1, much of the short-term capital inflow is "covered" in the forward exchange market against the risk of a change in the exchange rate. This complicates matters further, since one consequence of an increased capital inflow is to drive down the forward price of the Canadian dollar; the more the forward rate gives way, the less downward pressure results on the short-term exchange rate. Actually, this further interdependence proved a help to us in estimating

[13]Thomas A. Wilson, *Capital Investment and the Cost of Capital: A Dynamic Analysis*, Studies of the Royal Commission on Taxation, No. 30, Ottawa, Queen's Printer, 1967, pp. 76–9. Elasticities of the same order of magnitude are computed by Rudolf R. Rhomberg, "A Model of the Canadian Economy under Fixed and Fluctuating Exchange Rates," *Journal of Political Economy*, LXXII, Feb. 1964, pp. 9–10.
[14]Lawrence B. Smith, *The Postwar Canadian Residential Mortgage Market and the Role of Government*, unpublished Ph.D. thesis, Harvard University, 1966, pp. 168, 200–09.

INTERNATIONAL CAPITAL FLOWS ON CATEGORIES OF CANADIAN DOMESTIC EXPENDITURE

(flow figures in millions of 1957 dollars, quarterly rates)

International capital flow		Interest rate		Expenditure variable	Time period (quarter)					
Variable	Amount of change^a	Variable	Amount of change (percentage points)^b		1	2	3	4	5	6
U.S. direct investment	100	—	—	Business fixed investment	100^c / 27^d	100 / 27	100 / 27	0 / 0	0 / 0	0 / 0
Net portfolio^e	132 / 39 / 13	Corporate / Long-term government	−0.1	Business fixed investment	1.2^f / 0^g	2.2 / 0	2.8 / 17.3	3.0 / 12.2	2.8 / 0	2.3 / 0
Net portfolio^e	132 / 39 / 13	Long-term government	−0.1	Residential construction	1.8^h	2.7	4.2	2.5	0.8	0
Total short term	36 / 27 / 17	Short-term government	−0.1	Consumer durables	2.9	0	0	0	0	0

^aWhere multiple estimates appear, they correspond to differences in assumed economic conditions, or to differing statistical biases in the estimates, or both. See text.

^bIn constructing this table, we have chosen a reduction in the interest rate of one-tenth of one percent as the arbitrary factor setting the size of the capital-inflow disturbance (except in the case of direct investment, where no interest rate is involved). The estimated capital inflows are the amounts necessary to bring about this reduction, and the estimated expenditure changes are its results.

^cThis line pertains to periods of full employment.

^dThis line pertains to periods of less than full employment.

^eNet new issues of securities plus trade in outstanding securities.

^fThis line uses T. A. Wilson's estimates of the response of manufacturing investment to changes in the corporate bond rate; it assumes the applicability of Shirley Almon's lags for the United States to Canada, and that the elasticity estimated for the manufacturing sector applies to the whole of gross business capital formation.

^gThis line uses Rudolf Rhomberg's estimates of the response of non-residential construction and machinery and equipment investment to the government bond rate.

^hResidential construction expenditures in the first period are associated with the financing of construction through trade in outstanding securities; the remaining expenditure changes reflect the impact of a lower interest rate on mortgage approvals, taking the lag between approval and construction into account (based on L. B. Smith's estimates).

Source: See text.

the influence of a short-term capital disturbance on Canadian interest rates. Table II gives a range of estimates of the size of the capital inflow necessary to depress the Canadian short rate by one-tenth of one percent. The needed inflow would be least if the forward exchange rate is assumed to be unaffected by the inflow, and thus absorbs none of the inflow's influence. It would be most if the forward market adjusts fully, eliminating any remaining possibility for lenders to profit from covered interest arbitrage. The intermediate figure represents our best guess, based on the actual behaviour of the Canadian short-term interest and forward exchange rates over 1951–62.

The evidence available on the impact of short-term interest rates on expenditure in Canada is very limited. Economists often expect that this interest rate will govern the rate of business inventory accumulation, since businesses often borrow at short-term to finance the holding of inventories. The absolute size of the influence reported by Courchene is quite small,[15] and we were able to detect no significant influence in our own simple experiments. We did, however, find two other connections between short-term finance and real expenditure in Canada. Finance-company borrowing has been a significant component of Canadian capital inflows during the past decade, suggesting that increased inflows might ease consumer credit terms in Canada and cause higher spending on consumer durable goods. We did observe this influence, and also some indication that increased sales abroad of outstanding securities (this we treat as a short-term capital flow) are used by households to finance equities in residential construction. The apparent response of these expenditure categories to a drop in the short-term interest rate is reported in Table II.

C. DOMESTIC EXPENDITURE AND THE CURRENT-ACCOUNT BALANCE

We have tracked the influence of a capital-flow disturbance as far as the associated change in Canadian domestic expenditure. It now must be pursued on to the induced change in the current-account balance. For this we need "multipliers" describing the consequences of the expenditure changes that we have already calculated. The consequences generally include some additional increases in domestic expenditure and more or less proportional increases in spending on imports of goods and services.

Estimates of the response of income and the current-account balance to a domestic expenditure disturbance are readily found; indeed, the question

[15]T. J. Courchene, "Inventory Behavior and the Stock-Order Distinction: An Analysis by Industry and by Stage of Fabrication with Empirical Applications to the Canadian Manufacturing Sector," *Canadian Journal of Economics and Political Science*, XXXIII, Aug. 1967, pp. 325–57.

is, which to believe? A common output of present-day applied economics is the statistical model of national income determination in the short run. Those available for Canada contain as many as 50 equations describing the determinants of various components of income, expenditure, employment, the price level, etc. A principal feature of such models is that, after statistical estimates have been developed of relations (or parameters) embedded in each individual equation, the whole system can be solved. The solution describes the impact of a change in any exogenous variable (not explained within the model) on any variable that is endogenous (explained within the model). An example of such multiplier relations might be the impact of a change in government purchases of goods and services on the level of goods and services imports. These multipliers not only describe the effect of the change in the time period when the disturbance occurs, but also predict the path that the endogenous variable will follow in time periods subsequent to the disturbance. In doing so, they take into account all the adjustments that would go on in the economy during such a process—so far as the model has correctly captured the behavioural properties of the economy.

We made principal use of three such models. Two of them, by Rhomberg and Officer, employ quarterly data and concentrate on describing Canada's participation in the international economy.[16] May's model is based on annual data and concentrates on relations governing fiscal policy.[17] They are similar to one another in a general way, agreeing on the process of income determination and on most of the determinants of the behaviour of individual sectors of the economy. Nonetheless, the small differences remaining in the specification of their relationships can (and do) produce large proportional differences in their estimates of particular multipliers. The problem is particularly acute for the "dynamic multipliers" which describe the course of adjustment that a variable follows after it has been disturbed. They depend closely on how dynamic relationships have been specified in the underlying model—relationships between variables at different points in time. Economists are in substantial agreement about the static determinants of economic activity—what causes what, after everything has had time to work itself out. But they have

[16]Rhomberg, "A Model of the Canadian Economy"; Lawrence H. Officer, *An Econometric Model of Canada under the Fluctuating Exchange Rate*, Harvard Economic Studies, No. 130, Cambridge, Harvard University Press, 1968. Also see Rhomberg's "Effects of Exchange Depreciation in Canada, 1960–64," Economic Council of Canada, *Conference on Stabilization Policies*, Ottawa, Queen's Printer, 1966, pp. 99–125.
[17]Sydney May, "Dynamic Multipliers and Their Use for Fiscal Decision-Making," *Conference on Stabilization Policies*, pp. 155–87. Also see T. M. Brown, "A Forecast Determination of National Product, Employment, and Price Level in Canada, from an Econometric Model," National Bureau of Economic Research, Conference on Research in Income and Wealth, *Models of Income Determination*, Studies in Income and Wealth, Vol. 28, Princeton, Princeton University Press, 1964, pp. 59–86.

not worked out accurate measures of the *rates* at which variables respond to one another.[18] Hence we must remain sceptical about the accuracy of all dynamic multipliers except those that have been tested and proved successful for short-term forecasting—and no models of the Canadian economy fall into this class.

Consider the predictions that Rhomberg's and Officer's models supply for the effect of a $100-million change in government purchases of goods and services. Officer predicts that after two years real GNP will have increased by $210 million; Rhomberg predicts an increase of 50 percent more ($325 million). Officer expects money GNP (i.e., including the induced change in the general price level) to rise by $265 million; Rhomberg expects it to rise by more than four times as much ($1,165 million)! Officer's multipliers indicate that the current-account balance will worsen by $91 million, Rhomberg's by $236 million. It was beyond the scope of our own project to pick between these two sets of estimates on anything but an impressionistic basis. We opted for Officer's multipliers,[19] making adjustment for what we feel is an excessively long delay built into one of Officer's equations between changes in income and induced changes in capital formation.

D. ARE CAPITAL TRANSFERS REQUITED?

We have now assembled the materials necessary to disclose the impact of disturbances in international capital flows on the Canadian current-account balance. Table III was calculated by supposing an increase of $100 to occur in each category of capital inflow, this higher level to be sustained in each of the succeeding quarters. The figures show our estimate of the resulting change in the current account. A capital inflow would be just requited (with the generally favourable consequences that implies for domestic stability) if the induced current-account change settles down to be around $100.

It is clear that none of the income effects hit very close to the target. With full employment, an inflow of direct investment would be overrequited within a year and tend to produce a payments deficit. With heavy unemployment (or a high proportion of takeovers), however, it would be underrequited. We would guess that in what have been average conditions for

---

[18]This is not due to disagreements in principle about the time-shape of the relations. Rather, any arbitrarily chosen lag structure usually gives fairly good statistical results, and alternative lag structures simply have not been tested in competition with one another.

[19]For his one-period impact multipliers, see Officer, *An Econometric Model of Canada*, chap. 4; dynamic multipliers from this model appear in Caves and Reuber, *Capital Transfers*, Appendix C. Rhomberg's model indicates both unreasonably high rates of price increase and implicit marginal propensities to import.

TABLE III

ESTIMATES OF CUMULATIVE RESPONSE OF CURRENT ACCOUNT OF CANADIAN BALANCE
OF PAYMENTS TO EXOGENOUS DISTURBANCES IN CAPITAL INFLOWS
(dollars)

Type of disturbance	Time period (quarter)						
	1	2	3	4	5	6	7
1. Increase direct investment by $100							
(a) Full-employment conditions	25.6	51.2	83.6	105.7	145.0	192.9	236.6
(b) Less than full employment	6.9	13.8	22.6	28.5	39.2	52.1	63.9
2. Increase portfolio capital inflow by $100							
(a) Due to U.S. interest-rate fall	6.2	10.0	15.4	16.9	20.8	25.4	29.2
(b) Best guess[a]	2.1	3.3	5.1	5.6	6.9	8.5	9.7
(c) Minimum effect[b]	0.6	0.9	1.4	1.6	1.9	2.4	2.7
3. Increase short-term capital inflow by $100							
(a) No forward-rate change[c]	4.6	4.6	5.8	8.6	11.6	14.4	16.4
(b) Best guess[d]	2.9	2.9	3.7	5.7	7.3	9.1	10.3
(c) Full forward-rate change[c]	2.2	2.2	2.8	4.0	5.5	6.8	7.8
4. Reduce U.S. corporate liquidity by $100							
(a) Average U.S. conditions	0	0	0.5	0.6	0.7	0.7	0.7
(b) U.S. moderate unemployment	0	0	0.9	1.1	1.3	1.2	1.3

[a]Two-stage least-squares estimate of effect of autonomous disturbance in net new issues of
securities.
[b]Ordinary least-squares estimate of effect of autonomous disturbance in net new issues of
securities; statistical biases known to yield minimum estimate of effect.
[c]Forward exchange rate assumed, respectively, to be unaffected by exogenous changes in
short-term capital inflows and to adjust completely to eliminate profitable covered interest
arbitrage.
[d]Estimated typical behaviour of forward exchange rate.
Source: See text.

Canada in the post-World War II period—average level of employment,
industry mix of investment destinations, etc.—income effects just about
requite changes in direct investment, but they can fall on either side. Portfolio investment, concentrating on the line that represents our best guess,
would be underrequited by a wide margin, tending to leave a balance of
payments surplus. These figures are consistent with the coincidence often
noted between the high rates of portfolio capital inflow to Canada in the late
1950s and the high price of the Canadian dollar at that time. Even if our
numbers underestimate by half the "true" response of the current account
to portfolio disturbances, they would still be underrequited by a wide margin.
Short-term capital disturbances have about the same result as changes in
portfolio inflows, being underrequited by a wide margin. We feel certain
that the current-account adjustments in this case are seriously understated,

because of the grievously thin evidence available on the effect of Canadian short-term interest rates on domestic expenditure. But our result could nonetheless be multiplied by a very large adjustment factor without upsetting the qualitative conclusions. Furthermore, the forward exchange rate has shown more and more tendency to respond to capital-flow changes, moving to eliminate the possibility of profitable covered interest arbitrage. This trend reduces the income response expected from a disturbance in short-term capital flows.

We have concentrated so far entirely on income adjustments within the Canadian economy. It takes two to make a capital transfer, however, and income increases induced in Canada by increased flows may well correspond to decreases in the lending country, typically the United States. A fall in U.S. income reduces purchases from Canada (and possibly improves the supply of imports available to Canadians), and this adds to the current-account deterioration due to income changes in Canada. Line 4 of Table III presents a very rough guess about the possible effect of a $100 capital transfer from the United States to Canada on the Canadian current-account balance, operating through U.S. income changes.[20] The U.S. economy's great size and self-sufficiency, as is often noted, causes the proportion of any expenditure change that spills over to her trading partners to be very small. Thus, the U.S. contribution to adjustment in the Canadian current account, following a change in capital flows between the two nations, is quite small despite the fact that a substantial portion of the spillover from any U.S. income change *does* affect Canada. It does not alter any of the preceding conclusions about the direction of the net disturbance to the balance of payments.

E. ARE CAPITAL TRANSFERS INFLATIONARY?

We noted above that a capital disturbance could, according to simple theory of income determination, be just requited by income effects and still be, on

---

[20]The following sources were employed: effect of reduction in corporate liquidity on business capital formation, J. R. Meyer and R. R. Glauber, *Investment Decisions, Economic Forecasting, and Public Policy*, Boston, Division of Research, Graduate School of Business Administration, Harvard University, 1964, chap. 7; effect of expenditure change on gross national product, Gary Fromm and Paul Taubman, *Policy Simulations with an Econometric Model*, Washington, Brookings Institution, 1968, p. 48; marginal propensities to import, R. J. Ball and K. Marwah, "The U.S. Demand for Imports, 1948–1958," *Review of Economics and Statistics*, XLIV, Nov. 1962, pp. 395–401; direct and indirect effect of U.S. import change on Canadian current account, R. Piekarz and L. E. Stekler, "Induced Changes in Trade and Payments," *Review of Economics and Statistics*, XLIX, Nov. 1967, pp. 517–26.

balance, inflationary for the domestic economy. It is clear that direct investment disturbances have, on balance, tended to change Canadian employment in the direction of the disturbance—raising it when inflows increase,
reducing it when they fall. What about the other inflows, which we found to
be typically underrequited?

As the figures in Table II indicated, an increase in any type of capital
inflow has the direct effect of increasing domestic expenditure. The trouble
is that, with a flexible exchange rate, it may also change the exchange rate
in a way that tends to reduce expenditure. An underrequited capital transfer
means that the increased demand for a nation's currency on the foreign
exchange markets is not fully offset by the increased supply of it resulting
from larger purchases of imports. This drives the exchange rate up; as it
rises, exports fall and imports are inflated further, and this worsening of
the trade balance tends to drag down domestic expenditure.

We assembled some estimates of this drag, allowing for the fact that
capital flows themselves help to offset any tendency for the exchange rate
to shift (although they do not continue to fight the change indefinitely).[21]
Stacking up the deflationary pull of exchange-rate appreciation against the
inflationary pressure of the spending encouraged directly by capital flows,
we found that foreign direct investment is normally inflationary, even in
circumstances where it may be underrequited. With a flexible exchange rate,
there is no cause for blocking direct investment inflows for fear that they
might prove deflationary, even when unemployment prevails. Portfolio
capital inflows likewise are inflationary when they are due to a general
decline in United States interest rates. Portfolio inflows due to other outside
disturbances, however, are probably deflationary, as are nearly all exogenous
increases in short-term capital flows, whatever their causes.

3. Income adjustments and economic stability
We opened this chapter by inquiring whether or not exogenous changes in
capital flows constituted an important source of disturbance to the Canadian
economy. We attempted a preliminary answer by showing that, relative to
disturbances stemming from the current account of the balance of payments
and the domestic economy, capital flows originated a relatively small portion
of the disturbances impinging on the Canadian balance of payments over the
1951–62 period. We then evaluated the net displacements in the balance of
payments and domestic income stream from those disturbances which do
occur in the capital accounts. We can return to the original question for a
more searching evaluation of capital flows as a source of disturbance, now

[21]For details see Cave and Reuber, *Capital Transfers*, chap. 7.

that we can measure their consequences and gauge their net effect. A given type of capital inflow might be underrequited, tending to produce a payments surplus; yet if bulges in it occur fortuitously when the economy would otherwise tend to run an over-all payments deficit, its net impact is to stabilize the balance of payments. On the other hand, if it typically increases when other events are producing payments surpluses, it is destabilizing. In short, we go beyond the *abstract* question of the stabilizing properties of a capital disturbance to the *historical* question of whether or not a given capital flow has typically stabilized the economy.

To explore whether or not capital disturbances and the income responses that they induce have tended to stabilize the Canadian balance of payments, we first developed a series of quarterly estimates of swings in the capital accounts *net* of the influence of shifts in Canadian domestic policy variables. This is roughly the same operation as was undertaken in connection with the lead-lag analysis reported at the start of this chapter, and was done separately for each major category of capital flow. Then we calculated the series of current-account disturbances that would result from each quarter's capital-account disturbance, for that quarter and a series of quarters into the future (using the figures from Table III). Finally, for each quarter, we added up the current-account changes stemming from current and previous capital-account disturbances, and compared that quarter's capital-account and current-account changes. In some quarters the two changes tend to offset each other; in some, they reinforce each other. On the average, over the period 1951–62, we found that the income adjustments tended slightly to stabilize disturbances to the balance of payments emanating from the capital account as a whole. They typically reduced these disturbances by 6.4 percent.

Direct investment, portfolio investment, and short-term flows were examined individually in the same way. The responses to short-term flows also were marginally stabilizing, although they cut the average capital disturbance by only 3.1 percent. But the income responses to both direct and portfolio investment were destabilizing, augmenting the over-all disturbance to the balance of payments by 21.7 and 2.0 percent, respectively.

How could the aggregate response of the current account to disturbances in the capital balance be more stabilizing than the response imputed to any of its components separately? The answer is that the different types of capital flows tend themselves to be mutually stabilizing, with an above-average long-term inflow typically associated with a below-average short-term flow, so that the aggregate forces operating on the balance of payments tend to come out right. Note that this accommodation of exogenous disturbances in the long and short flows did not operate through Canadian interest rates, for interest rates were among the policy variables whose influences we removed in deriving these estimates of exogenous disturbances. It operates through other channels. Possibly the explanation is simply the practice whereby Canadians who borrow abroad hold the proceeds initially in foreign currency, repatriating them only at a rate geared to desired rates of expenditure.

This analysis of exogenous capital inflows and their consequences for economic stability can be pushed one step farther by comparing these net pressures on the balance of payments with actual movements of the exchange rate. Assuming that our figures give a reasonably accurate account of pressures on the balance of payments due to capital disturbances, then we should have a measure of one factor pushing on the flexible exchange rate in each quarter. If the actual fluctuations of the rate match up closely with our calculated series of net disturbances, then we could conclude that capital disturbances were a significant source of instability in Canada's international payments. If not, then we could count them innocent of destabilizing influence—or perhaps suspect that our calculation of that influence itself is not too accurate! In any case we found no relation of any significance between the net disturbances and the exchange rate.

A good deal of work in economic theory has gone to trying to predict the consequences of just this sort of capital-account disturbance for a nation's terms of trade, the relation of the prices of internationally traded goods to those produced and consumed only at home, etc. All of this theory assumes that capital-account changes imprint a major disturbance on the foreign-exchange market and that this disturbance in turn effects a change in the terms of trade or other variables. But with no substantial external disturbance to work with—one strong enough to show its effect on the exchange rate— we found no ground for hunting further. This is not to deny that changes in *total* capital flows—not just those components which we have branded "exogenous"—might underlie shifts in domestic price relations. But these disturbances have domestic causes that may be linked to price adjustments through other connections than capital flows. That becomes another story.

3. The Influence of International Capital Flows on the Effectiveness of Domestic Policy Instruments

Since World War II successive governments in most countries have committed themselves to the fuller attainment of an ever-widening list of frequently conflicting economic objectives, at the same time that the international economy has become more highly interdependent and the scope for independent national policies has been narrowed. The resulting dilemmas have inspired an extensive and fast-growing literature concerned specifically with the theory and application of economic policy.[1] Among the many issues that have been examined are questions such as these: to what degree do objectives conflict with each other? What are the relationships among policy instruments and between instruments and objectives? How and to what benefit can the number of instruments be increased in relation to the number of goals? How can the effectiveness of existing policy instruments be improved? And how can the array of policy instruments at hand be combined in the most effective manner? Vexing as these questions remain within the context of a closed economy, they become substantially more complex when the discussion is extended to allow for the free international exchange of currently produced goods and services, on the one hand, and for the free international exchange of financial assets and liabilities, on the other. These international exchanges, corresponding to the current and capital sides of a country's balance of international payments, not only are responsive to domestic developments but also condition the manner in which the economy responds to changes in circumstances and policies.

This chapter is concerned with the opportunities and constraints that are created for domestic economic policy by closely integrated international capital markets implying highly mobile international capital flows. Specifically, how do capital flows respond to changes in policy and what implications does the responsiveness of international capital flows have for the

[1]Although many economists have of course addressed themselves to questions of economic policy through the years, scientific work in this area was greatly advanced and accelerated by the pioneering studies of James E. Meade, *The Balance of Payments*, London, Oxford University Press, 1951; H. Theil, *Economic Forecasts and Policy*, Amsterdam, North-Holland Publishing Company, 1958; and Jan Tinbergen, *The Theory of Economic Policy*, Amsterdam, North-Holland Publishing Company, 1952.

effectiveness of the instruments of policy in achieving policy objectives? We consider this question in relation to four major instruments of stabilization policy available to governments—monetary, fiscal, debt-management, and exchange-rate policy. These instruments remain the principal weaponry available in most countries with market-oriented economies for controlling the levels of income and employment and for regulating the rate of economic growth. In addition, each of these instruments is directly linked through financial markets to capital flows.

1. Domestic policy instruments and balance of payments adjustment

Although it is beyond the scope of this study to review the extensive literature that has developed on this subject, it will facilitate comprehension of our empirical findings if we begin with a brief sketch of the theoretical relationships between changes in economic policy and the process of balance of payments adjustment.[2] In discussing these relationships, we shall assume a situation where there is some unemployment in the economy, calling for expansionary policies. The adjustment process following in the wake of contractionary policies is simply the reverse of that entailed by expansionary policies and is not discussed separately.

A. MONETARY POLICY

Monetary policy affects the level of aggregate demand and unemployment by changing the cost and availability of credit. Suppose easier credit conditions are created or condoned by the authorities. In the absence of any international flows of capital and assuming normal market responses, interest rates decrease, credit is more readily available, spending can be expected to increase, and the current account can be expected to deteriorate. Under a fixed-exchange-rate system this means that foreign-exchange-reserve holdings either decrease more rapidly or accumulate more slowly than they otherwise would. What additional consequences this change in the balance

[2]Among the more important recent literature on this subject, the reader is referred to the following: William Fellner *et al., Maintaining and Restoring Balance in International Payments*, Princeton, New Jersey, Princeton University Press, 1966; J. M. Fleming, "Domestic Financial Policies under Fixed and under Floating Exchange Rates," *IMF Staff Papers*, IX, Nov. 1962, 369–79; Anne O. Krueger, "The Impact of Alternative Government Policies under Varying Exchange Systems," *Quarterly Journal of Economics*, LXXIX, May 1965, pp. 195–209; R. A. Mundell, "The Appropriate Use of Monetary and Fiscal Policy for Internal and External Stability," *IMF Staff Papers*, IX, March 1962, pp. 70–7, and "Capital Mobility and Stabilization Policy under Fixed and Flexible Exchange Rates," *Canadian Journal of Economics and Political Science*, XXIX, Nov. 1963, pp. 475–85; R. A. Mundell and A. K. Swoboda (eds.), *Monetary Problems of the International Economy*, Chicago, University of Chicago Press, 1968; Rudolf R. Rhomberg, "A Model of the Canadian Economy," pp. 1–31.

of payments position of the country has on the money supply and on spending will depend on how the deterioration in the reserve position affects the money supply. If changes in foreign-exchange-reserve holdings are "sterilized," in the sense that government receipts and payments associated with foreign-exchange transactions are prevented from affecting the size of the money supply, then the initiating change in the money supply remains intact, and its consequences via the adjustment process will be realized. If, on the other hand, a loss in reserves is permitted to reverse part of the initiating increase in the money supply, then the effectiveness of the initial change in monetary policy will be correspondingly reduced.

With a flexible exchange rate, as the current account deteriorates in response to the easing of credit conditions, the rate tends to depreciate, thereby discouraging imports and stimulating exports and offsetting the initial income effect on the current-account balance. At the same time, the reduction in imports and the increase in exports resulting from the exchange-rate depreciation reduce the leakage out of the income circuits and raise the total increases in GNP and employment stemming from the initial easing of monetary policy.

If this relaxation, leading to a reduction in interest rates, results in a large exodus of foreign capital, this picture of the adjustment process is modified in two major respects. First, the induced outflow of capital will leave credit conditions tighter than they would have been in the absence of such an outflow. Consequently, the effect of a given change in the money supply—the monetary policy variable—on the level of spending will be less than it would have been without capital flows. Conversely, one may say that in order to attain a desired effect on domestic interest rates via monetary policy, the monetary instrument will have to be moved through a wider range, the more readily capital flows respond to interest-rate changes. And in a world of perfectly mobile international capital, monetary policy will be completely frustrated by capital flows, at least for any small or medium-sized country, in its efforts to change domestic interest rates relative to the level of rates prevailing internationally.

In addition to the direct link through international capital flows, the responsiveness of interest rates may also be affected by external influences on expectations. When capital markets are closely linked internationally and particularly when there are many other links as well and neighbouring countries are relatively large, expectations about the future of domestic interest rates may be closely linked to the level of interest rates externally. If so, the ability of the monetary authorities to pursue an independent interest-rate policy is further undermined.

Secondly, it is necessary to recognize the interdependence between capital flows and the balance of payments. If a country adheres to a fixed exchange rate, an outflow of capital in response to easier monetary policy will, *ceteris paribus*, reduce reserve holdings. Moreover, this reduction in reserves will have to be sterilized in the sense mentioned earlier if a retreat from the initial change in monetary policy is to be avoided. And although this may frequently not prove to be very difficult, if capital flows respond strongly enough (i.e., with infinite elasticity) to any tendency for the interest rate to change, it may prove literally impossible. In that extreme case either monetary policy becomes completely ineffective or the exchange rate must give way. Canadian experience in the late 1940s with a fixed exchange rate illustrates the possibility that in some situations the authorities may find some difficulty in sterilizing very large changes in foreign-exchange reserves prompted by large-scale international capital movements.

If a country operates under a flexible-exchange-rate system, an outflow of capital in response to easier credit conditions will lead to a depreciation in the rate. This cheapening of the nation's currency will raise its exports and lower spending on imports. The resulting improvement in the current account acts on employment just like an increase in domestic investment. With the exchange rate flexible, monetary policy miraculously affects employment through this "outside" channel even if capital flows are so responsive that the domestic interest rate is locked in place. To look at it another way, monetary policy will work through some combination of this "outside" and the conventional "inside" channel via the interest rate, the mix depending on how elastic are capital flows.

Influence through the outside channel may encounter a roadblock, however. This arises from the responsiveness of capital flows to exchange-rate changes as described in chapter 1. If borrowers and lenders expect the rate to return to its initial level, any tendency for the exchange rate to depreciate will tend to discourage capital outflows and to encourage capital inflows because of the possibility of realizing capital gains. Such a response to exchange-rate changes will tend to stabilize the current level of exchange rate.[3] This means that the adjustment in domestic spending via exchange-rate movements will be less than it would be in the absence of capital responses to exchange-rate changes, since the exchange rate is rendered less responsive to changes in monetary policy. Indeed, it is conceivable that the expectation that the exchange rate will remain at its initial level is so strongly held that even though the country has a flexible-rate system, the exchange rate will in fact remain unchanged and, hence, that this outside route for

[3]The opposite would be true if lenders and borrowers expected further changes in the rate in the same direction. This implies an unstable foreign-exchange market—a possibility that we ignore.

monetary policy to alter the level of GNP will be completely blocked, just as if the authorities had fixed the rate.

In summary, one may say that highly mobile international capital flows can complicate monetary policy in several ways: (1) by reducing the direct effect of a given change in monetary policy on domestic interest rates and credit conditions; (2) if the exchange rate is fixed, by substantially enhancing any difficulties which may arise in sterilizing changes in foreign-exchange reserves and effecting the desired change in the money supply sought by the authorities; and (3) by curbing the movement of a flexible exchange rate and hence reducing the effect of monetary policy on GNP via exchange-rate changes. The team of monetary policy and a flexible rate is basically a winner, however. Interest-sensitive capital flows provide a new channel for the influencing of aggregate demand and employment. Even if this channel should in turn be blocked because capital flows are also sensitive to the exchange rate, the "inside" channel of monetary influence on aggregate demand is left unimpaired.

B. FISCAL POLICY

We identify changes in fiscal policy with changes in government expenditures and changes in taxes. Either way, changes in government policies influence capital flows through their effects on the government's deficit and hence on the size of the public debt. The impact of fiscal policy on employment is altered from what it would be without capital movements.

Assume, as before, that there are no foreign capital flows. An easing of fiscal policy through an increase in government expenditure or a reduction in taxes or both will increase GNP which, in turn, will worsen the current-account balance. As a consequence, under a fixed exchange rate the level of foreign-exchange reserves will be reduced; alternatively, a flexible exchange rate under this same pressure will depreciate, so that imports will tend to decrease and exports to increase. As with monetary policy, the leakage from the income circuit is reduced and the leverage of fiscal policy on employment increased by this induced improvement in the current account.

At the same time, however the exchange rate is managed, the increase in the government's budgetary deficit as a consequence of undertaking an expansionary fiscal policy, together with the greater demand for credit as GNP expands, will tend to raise interest rates and generally tighten credit conditions, *given the quantity of money*.[4] This tightening of monetary condi-

[4]Here and in the remainder of this chapter we abstract from any complications that may arise in sterilizing changes in foreign-exchange reserves.

tions will tend to curb domestic spending and therefore will offset to some extent the expansionary expenditure effects of easier fiscal policy. It has generally been assumed that the reduction in the leverage of fiscal policy on GNP because of the adverse monetary effects associated with fiscal policy changes are relatively unimportant in the absence of capital flows, since there is considerable evidence to suggest that the effects of associated changes in interest rates and credit conditions on domestic spending are weak in comparison with the expenditure effects of fiscal changes.

This picture is modified considerably when we allow for highly mobile international capital flows. The monetary effects of easier fiscal policy, raising interest rates and making credit less readily available, will serve to attract capital inflows. With a fixed rate these induced capital inflows will enlarge foreign-exchange reserves, thereby offsetting to some degree the drain on reserves arising from the deterioration in the current account associated with the expansion of GNP. In a world of perfectly mobile capital flows, capital would continue to flow into the country until the interest-decreasing effects of the capital inflow offset the interest-increasing effects of the easing of fiscal policy. The extent of the change in foreign-exchange reserves would depend on the relative strength of these two opposing forces. In any case, the adverse monetary side effects of fiscal policy are offset, and its efficiency for raising employment improved.

Under a flexible exchange rate, as capital flows into the country in response to the tighter monetary conditions created by easier fiscal policy, upward pressure will be exerted on the exchange rate—in opposition to the downward pressure on the rate emanating from the expansionary expenditure effects of easier fiscal policy. The more elastic are these capital flows, the more likely is the upward pull of capital flows on the exchange rate to prevail, worsening the current account and depressing employment. In the extreme, the favourable direct effect of fiscal policy on expenditure can be completely offset by the adverse influence of exchange-rate appreciation on the current account. If capital flows are also sensitive to the exchange rate, however, this frustration will be somewhat relieved. Here, blocking the "outside" channel helps the effectiveness of fiscal policy, just as it hampered the effectiveness of monetary policy.

Until recently it had usually been assumed that the expenditure effects of fiscal policy would outweigh the monetary effects by a considerable margin and, therefore, that easier fiscal policy would be associated with exchange-rate depreciation or a reduction in foreign-exchange holdings. An important empirical study by Rudolf Rhomberg has called this assumption into serious question. Rhomberg's results suggest that the monetary consequences of fiscal policy changes outweigh the expenditure consequences and that under a flexible-rate system the exchange rate is likely to appreciate in the face of an easier fiscal policy.[5]

The main conclusion of all this from the standpoint of economic policy is that capital-market integration, which provides the basis for highly mobile capital flows, diminishes the effectiveness of a given change in fiscal policy under a flexible-exchange-rate system. Without capital flows, exchange-rate adjustments would more strongly reinforce the direct effects of expenditure policy. Under a fixed-rate system, on the other hand, mobile capital flows increase the effectiveness of fiscal policy. This is because capital flows tend to eliminate the adverse monetary effects of fiscal policy on domestic spending and to reduce the change in foreign-exchange reserves. This is particularly important in the case of expansionary, as compared to contractionary, fiscal policy changes, since losses in foreign-exchange reserves are more likely, on past experience, to set a limit to how far expansionary fiscal policies can be pursued than are reserve accumulations.

C. DEBT-MANAGEMENT POLICY

Debt-management policy is concerned with the time-to-maturity distribution of the public debt. For our purpose changes in debt-management policy are measured statistically by changes in the average term to maturity (ATM) of the total debt (excluding money) of the government. The specific issue in question is what effect a change in ATM has on GNP with or without capital flows and with or without a fixed exchange rate.

A change in ATM influences GNP by altering both the term structure and the level of interest rates as well as the availability of credit. Consequently, it is similar in many respects to changes in monetary policy. We make the conventional assumption, without arguing its validity, that a decrease in ATM tends to reduce interest rates generally and to reduce long-term rates relative to short-term rates.[6] To the extent that debt-management policy changes the general level of interest rates, the analysis corresponds exactly to that already outlined in connection with monetary policy, and no more needs to be said. It remains to consider briefly those aspects of debt-management policy associated with a shift in the term structure of rates.

Suppose long-term rates decrease relative to short-term rates. This may be expected to stimulate domestic spending for at least two reasons: the country is rendered more liquid as it shifts from long- to short-term securities

[5]Rhomberg, "A Model of the Canadian Economy."
[6]This assumption is consistent with our empirical evidence for Canada for the period from 1952 to 1961.

in response to the relative change in rates; and the relative reduction in long-term rates may have a greater leverage on decisions to invest if only because of interest-cost considerations. In the absence of international capital flows, the increase in GNP and the deterioration in the current account that are likely to be associated with a reduction in long-term rates relative to short-term rates will result in downward pressure either on exchange reserves or on the exchange rate. The effect of these responses on the leverage on GNP of debt management was outlined in connection with monetary and fiscal policy. In the case of mobile capital flows, any scope that may exist to alter the term structure of interest rates domestically will be considerably impaired, depending on the responsiveness of capital flows. Any tendency for long-term rates to fall relative to short-term rates domestically will tend to be offset by countervailing movements in long- and short-term capital (abstracting still from the general level of rates). At the extreme, the domestic structure of rates will simply be a mirror image of the international structure of rates.[7] If we assume that capital flows are sticky enough to make it feasible to reduce long-term rates relative to short-term rates domestically, given the international structure of rates, the net response on capital account will depend on the responsiveness of capital flows in different segments of the maturity spectrum of the securities market and on the extent to which debt-management policy exerts pressures on the different segments of this market. Without specifying these responses, it is not clear whether, as a result of a reduction in long- relative to short-term rates, capital on balance will flow out or into the country, considering only these substitution effects. If, however, we add the realistic assumption that a reduction in ATM is accompanied by a reduction in the general *level* of rates, it is apparent that a reduction in ATM will lead to a net outflow of capital.

This outflow of capital will add further downward pressure on the foreign-exchange holdings or the exchange rate in addition to that arising from the increased domestic expenditures associated with a reduction in ATM. How much the exchange rate depreciates under a flexible rate under the combined domestic and external pressures on the rate will depend on the counter-vailing pressure for capital to flow into the country, because of expectations about the future level of the rate, as the exchange rate depreciates. To the extent that the exchange rates does in fact depreciate, imports will be curbed and exports will be increased, thereby enhancing GNP and reinforcing the

[7] Even without foreign capital flows, it is an open question whether the term structure of rates can be much affected by altering the length of the debt. If one assumes complete mobility of funds between various sectors of the market and explains long-term rates in terms of expected short-term rates, the term structure of the rate is largely independent of the length of the debt. See David Meiselman, *The Term Structure of Interest Rates*, Englewood Cliffs, New Jersey, Prentice-Hall, 1962.

effect on GNP attributable to the domestic expenditure effects of the reduction in ATM.

In short, with highly mobile capital flows, a country's ability to maintain not only an independent *level* of interest rates but also an independent *structure* of interest rates is impaired, thereby undermining whatever effectiveness debt management may have as an instrument of stabilization policy. Under a flexible-exchange-rate system, however, some extra leverage on domestic spending may be gained through exchange-rate adjustments. How great this extra leverage is depends partly on how stable the exchange rate remains in the face of expectations about the future of the rate.

2. Canadian experience: 1952 to 1961

Although economic theory predicts the general direction of the effects that mobile capital flows exert on the adjustment process, it cannot indicate the magnitude of these effects. This is an empirical question that depends on the relative size of a variety of responses to changes in policy. Canada, because of the high degree of integration between its capital market and that of the United States, because of its experience with a flexible exchange rate from 1952 to 1961, and because of the availability of empirical estimates pertaining to some of the important relationships in question, offers unique possibilities for examining the effect of capital flows on the leverages of the major instruments of stabilization policy. The empirical estimates on which we have drawn particularly heavily are those derived from the model of the Canadian economy fitted by Lawrence H. Officer.[8] These estimates, together with our own empirical investigations, enable us to establish the orders of magnitude in question with some assurance, even though we make no claim to having estimated these relationships with precision.

A. RESPONSES TO MONETARY POLICY

In order to estimate the influence of international capital flows on the effectiveness of Canadian monetary policy, we pose the following question: given the relationships prevailing from 1952 to 1961, how did Canada's GNP, balance of payments, and exchange rate respond to an increase of 1 percent in the rate of growth in the money supply, and how would they have responded in the absence of international capital responses? From the answer

[8]Officer, *An Econometric Model of Canada Under the Fluctuating Exchange Rate.* Other estimates that were considered were those provided by Rhomberg, "A Model of the Canadian Economy"; May, "Dynamic Multipliers," pp. 155–87; and the *Report of the Royal Commission on Taxation*, Ottawa, Queen's Printer, 1966, vol. 2. The flexible exchange rate actually prevailed from late 1950 to 1962, but transitional disturbances forced us to base our findings on the shorter period.

to this question we may infer to what extent the effectiveness of monetary policy was affected by capital flows and exchange-rate variations.

In order to keep track of all the complicated relationships in play, it will be helpful to begin by considering the relationship between interest rates and capital flows, abstracting for the moment from exchange-rate considerations.[9] Our estimates suggest that, in the absence of international capital flows, a 1 percent increase in the rate of growth in the Canadian money supply during the 1950s could have been expected to reduce long-term interest rates by approximately 0.06 to 0.10 percentage points. When allowance is made for capital flows, this picture is altered quite substantially. As indicated in chapter 2, our estimates indicate that the elasticity of portfolio capital with respect to interest-rate changes ranges from 6.0 to 10.6; our best estimate is probably 9.1. Direct investment was also responsive to interest-rate changes, though much less so; our figures suggest an elasticity coefficient for this category of capital of about 1.4. Given this responsiveness, as monetary policy put downward pressure on interest rates, capital was withdrawn from the country, thereby alleviating some of the pressure on rates. As a consequence, the actual reduction in rates ranged from 92 to 54 percent, according to our estimates, of the reduction in rates that would have occurred in the absence of capital flows. Our best estimate is that the decline in rates was about two-thirds of what it would otherwise have been. Putting it another way, one can say that the efficiency of monetary policy in terms of its impact on interest rates was reduced by perhaps one-third by international capital flows: at a minimum it was reduced by about a tenth and at a maximum by almost a half.

These estimates all assume that the only way international capital flows affected Canadian interest rates was through their effect on the supply of credit. If we go a step further and assume that the integration of capital markets makes it likely that expectations about long-term interest rates in Canada are based on long-term interest rates in the United States, we find that the efficiency of monetary policy was impaired substantially more. This second channel of influence presumably is what is meant by such remarks as "Canadian interest rates are made in Washington." Our evidence for Canada is consistent with the view that during the 1950s Canadian interest rates were closely linked to long-term U.S. interest rates via expectations—more closely than to expectations about future short-term rates in Canada. When allowance is made for this direct link with U.S. rates, we find that, in response to

[9]Details concerning the derivation of the estimates on the responsiveness of capital flows to changes in interest rates and exchange rates and the responsiveness of interest rates and exchange rates to capital flows are given in Caves and Reuber, *International Capital Flows*, chaps. 2 and 3.

a 1 percent increase in the money supply, long-term interest rates decreased only 0.01 to 0.02 percentage points.

Short-term capital flows are also highly responsive to interest rates, with elasticity coefficients on the order of 8 or 9. Apparently the response of short-term capital flows to easier monetary policy and interest-rate reductions would have wiped out between 33 and 93 percent of the decrease in short-term rates that would have occurred in the absence of highly mobile capital flows. The lower estimate assumes that the forward exchange rate was directly linked to the spot rate of exchange via the differential between short-term interest rates in Canada and the United States and that the relationship between the forward and the spot rate was kept continuously in equilibrium through interest-rate arbitrage. The upper estimate assumes that the forward rate was determined independently of interest-rate differentials between the two countries. Our best estimate is based on the assumption of a link between the forward and the spot rates via the interest differential but allows for some variation in the forward rate that is independent of the spot rate and the interest differential. This allowance is made on the basis of a direct estimate of the determinants of the forward rate from 1952 to 1961. Calculated in this manner, our best estimate indicates that between 45 and 57 percent—one-half in round numbers—of the effect of changes in monetary policy on short-term interest rates was wiped out by compensating flows of short-term capital.

Table IVA presents a summary of our evidence on the effect of a change in monetary policy on interest rates with and without international capital flows. Table IVB shows our estimates of the movements of capital which served to curb the effect of the assumed change in monetary policy on interest rates. These capital-flow estimates drop out of the same calculations as those on which the interest-rate estimates are based, since the estimates allow for interaction between interest rates and capital flows. The capital flows, it should be recognized, were considerably less than they would have been had interest rates decreased by the full amount implied by the easing of monetary policy *prior* to allowing for the effect of capital outflows in curbing the decrease in interest rates. In considering Tables IVA and IVB, it should also be remembered that these estimates make no allowance for exchange-rate movements.

Before proceeding to consider the effects of monetary policy on GNP and the balance of payments, there is a related aspect of the adjustments we have been discussing that warrants mention. A question frequently asked in Canada is how independent are Canadian interest rates from U.S. interest rates, given the high degree of capital mobility between the two countries. In round numbers our estimates show that between 10 and 80 percent of any

TABLE IVA

INFLUENCE OF CAPITAL MOBILITY ON EFFECTS OF AN INCREASE OF 1 PERCENT IN THE RATE OF GROWTH
OF THE CANADIAN MONEY SUPPLY ON INTEREST RATES

	Long-term rates		Short-term rates	
	Range	Best estimate	Range	Best estimate
Change in interest rates, percentage points				
1. Without capital flows	−0.06 to −0.10	−0.10		
2. With capital flows				
(a) No expectations effect	−0.04 to −0.07	−0.06	−0.04 to −0.09	−0.08
(b) Expectations linked to U.S. rates	−0.01	−0.01	No direct estimate	
Percentage loss in independence because of capital flows				
3. No expectations effect	10 to 46	33	33 to 93	55
4. Expectations linked to U.S. rates	80	80	No direct estimate	

Source: Caves and Reuber, *Capital Transfers, op. cit.*, chaps. 2 and 3.

TABLE IVB

ESTIMATED CAPITAL FLOWS ASSOCIATED WITH AN INCREASE OF 1 PERCENT IN THE RATE OF GROWTH
OF THE CANADIAN MONEY SUPPLY*
($ million)

	Portfolio capital		Short-term capital	
	Range	Best estimate	Range	Best estimate
No expectations effect	−24 to −45	−41	−23 to −34	−32
Expectations linked to U.S. rates	−4	−4	No direct estimates	

Source: Caves and Reuber, *Capital Transfers*, *op. cit.*, chaps. 2 and 3.
*The capital-flow estimates correspond to the estimated changes in interest rates shown in Table IVA.

change in U.S. interest rates during the 1950s was passed on to long-term rates in Canada, assuming that the Canadian monetary authorities did not undertake offsetting policies. The upper estimate assumes that Canadian interest rates are linked to U.S. rates not only through capital flows but also through expectations. Our best estimate, leaving expectations aside, is that about a third of the change in U.S. rates was reflected in Canadian long-term rates, assuming that Canadian policy was passive. For short-term rates the estimated loss in independence ranges from 33 to 90 percent; our best estimate is 55 percent. These estimates are shown in lines 3 and 4 of Table IVA.

Though capital movements tempered the change in interest rates associated with easier monetary policy, some decrease in rates did occur which affected the level of spending and GNP. These changes, however, manifest themselves more slowly over time because of lags between changes in interest rates and spending; our evidence indicates that the interaction between interest rates and capital flows worked itself out in the same quarter as the change in monetary policy. Table II shows estimated relationships between interest-rate changes and changes in various categories of investment for six quarters following the change in interest rates. Combining these estimates with the interest-rate changes summarized in Table IV and multiplier estimates derived from Officer's model, we calculated the effect on GNP and the current account of a 1 percent increase in the rate of growth of the money supply. The sum of this current-account change and the capital-account change resulting from the reduction in interest rates provides an estimate of the net change in the balance of payments without exchange-rate adjustments—in other words, an estimate of the net change in reserve holdings had Canada been on a fixed-exchange-rate system from 1952 to 1961.

This combination of estimates is summarized in part A of Table V, showing our most likely as well as minimum and maximum estimates. These minima and maxima are based on the range of estimated responses of interest rates and capital flows to the assumed change in monetary policy. Here, as elsewhere in this study, the impact effect of a policy change is identified with changes in the current quarter (quarter 1 in the tables), and longer-term effects with changes in subsequent quarters. Without exchange-rate adjustments our best estimate indicates that, as a result of increasing the rate of growth of the money supply by 1 percent, GNP could be expected to increase by $4.3 million immediately and additional increases of roughly comparable size could be expected over the next year and a half. The current-account balance could be expected to deteriorate by $1.1 million immediately, followed by further deterioration in subsequent quarters. The greatest change occurs in the capital account, which could be expected to deteriorate by

TABLE V

SIZE AND TIMING OF THE EFFECTS OF A 1 PERCENT INCREASE IN THE RATE OF GROWTH OF THE MONEY SUPPLY ON GNP, THE BALANCE OF PAYMENTS, AND EXCHANGE RATES ($ million)

	Quarters					
	1	2	3	4	5	6
A. *Without exchange-rate adjustments*						
1. Change in GNP						
(a) Best estimate	4.3	3.3	5.0	4.9	4.5	4.4
(b) Minimum estimate	1.5	0.6	1.0	1.0	0.9	0.9
(c) Maximum estimate	5.0	3.9	6.1	5.8	5.4	5.3
2. Change in the balance of payments						
(a) Best estimate:						
current account	-1.1	-0.8	-1.3	-1.6	-1.9	-2.2
capital account	-73.0					
total	-74.1					
(b) Minimum estimate	-27.4	-0.8	-1.3	-1.6	-1.9	-2.2
(c) Maximum estimate	-80.3	-0.9	-1.5	-1.9	-2.3	-2.7
B. *With exchange-rate adjustments*						
3. Change in GNP						
(a) Best estimate	63.8	7.1	13.2	17.1	18.8	19.0
(b) Minimum estimate	14.0	1.4	2.6	3.6	3.9	4.0
(c) Maximum estimate	70.0	8.1	14.9	19.3	21.1	21.4
4. Change in exchange rate (cents)						
(a) Best estimate	-0.6151	-0.0044	-0.0072	-0.0088	-0.0105	-0.0121
(b) Minimum estimate	-0.1290	-0.0007	-0.0014	-0.0020	-0.0024	-0.0027
(c) Maximum estimate	-0.6715	-0.0050	-0.0084	-0.0105	-0.0124	-0.0147

Source: Caves and Reuber, *Capital Transfers op. cit.*, Tables 8.7 and 8.8.

about $73 million immediately. This means that the impact of the change in monetary policy would be a deterioration in the balance of payments of $74.1 million, on the basis of our best estimate, followed by further but much more modest deterioration in subsequent quarters ranging from $0.8 to $2.2 million.

As explained earlier, these figures assume that the authorities sterilize changes in exchange reserves in the sense of not allowing such changes to feed back on the size of the money supply. If the authorities fail to sterilize the change in reserves, the drain of exchange reserves arising from the deterioration in the balance of payments will lead to a reversal of the easier monetary policy that initiated the whole process. How far this reversal goes depends on how firmly the authorities control the money supply.

If, instead of assuming adjustments in exchange reserves, we assume that balance of payments pressures are reflected in the exchange rate, as in fact occurred during the 1950s in Canada, the increase in external payments on both current and capital account will lead to a depreciation in the exchange rate. As a consequence, domestic output will gain a price advantage relative to imports domestically and relative to the production of other countries in export markets. This will dampen the deterioration in the current account. At the same time, the deterioration of the exchange rate will open the possibility of capital gains to investors if they expect the variation in the rate to be temporary and the long-run normal level of the rate to remain unchanged. On this assumption, depreciation of the rate will curb the net outflow of capital.

Our estimates indicate that during the period in question the elasticity of imports of goods and services with respect to price changes was at least 1.0 and the elasticity of exports of goods and services was at least 0.35. As for the capital account, our estimates of the elasticity of short-term capital flows with respect to exchange-rate changes range from 63 to 108. The estimated elasticity coefficients for long-term capital are somewhat less satisfactory, but these indicate that new portfolio issues also were quite responsive to exchange-rate changes. For this category of capital the estimated elasticity coefficients range from 6 to 33.

How much changes in the spot rate of exchange affected short-term capital flows depends on what we assume about the relationship between the forward and spot exchange rates and the differential between short-term interest rates in Canada and the United States. At one extreme we can assume that the forward rate is determined completely independently of the spot rate and the interest-rate differential, in which case our estimates indicate that a one-cent depreciation in the exchange rate called forth $35 million in short-term foreign capital. At the other extreme we may assume that the forward rate is determined entirely by the spot rate of exchange and the interest differential through interest-arbitrage operations, in which case a one-cent depreciation in the exchange rate evoked about $58 million in short-term capital from abroad, according to our estimates. Our best estimate, which allows for several influences on the forward rate in addition to the spot rate of exchange and the interest-rate differential, is that a depreciation in the exchange rate during this period led to an inflow of short-term capital of about $51 million. Our estimates also indicate that exchange-rate changes influenced long-term portfolio capital flows but had no discernible effect on direct investment. A one-cent depreciation in the exchange rate in the current quarter is associated with an inflow of portfolio capital in the next quarter of about $24 million. In addition to a lower response rate, this result differs from that for short-term capital in that short-term capital flows respond without a lag.

A further set of calculations provides estimates of the linkages between changes in various international payments categories and the exchange rate. Combining these with the estimated responses shown in line 2 of Table V, one can derive part B of Table V, which shows the effect of the assumed increase in the money supply on GNP and on the exchange rate under a flexible rate. As is evident from these figures, exchange-rate adjustments greatly enhance the effectiveness of monetary policy, particularly in the short run but also in the longer term. The extent of the adjustment implied by the estimates is indicated in line 4. Evidently the rate could be expected to depreciate initially by $0.0062; a year after the change in policy the rate would have depreciated $0.0064 and a year and a half later by $0.0066.

B. RESPONSES TO FISCAL POLICY

Fiscal policy affects GNP and the balance of payments through its influence on the total level of private and public expenditure. Expenditure changes may arise from changes in private investment, government outlays, the current-account balance, or consumption. For our purposes we have swept aside all complications arising from the diversity of responses that may be expected to follow from changes in various categories of expenditures and taxes. We assume that there are two categories of response. The first is the response of GNP and the current account to changes in investment spending, government outlays, and the current-account balance: these responses are assumed to be equal to the estimates derived from Officer's model.

According to these estimates an increase in government expenditure of $100 million, assuming the new level of expenditure to be maintained over time, can be expected to increase GNP immediately by $105 million and, after six quarters, by $190 million. At the same time the current account can be expected to deteriorate by $26 million immediately and by some $80 million after six quarters. If we assume that the money supply is fixed, this increase in GNP will be accompanied by an increase in interest rates, which, in turn, will improve the capital account. Given tax rates and the money supply, the government has to increase its borrowing from the public in order to finance the increase in its expenditures. Initially, virtually all the new expenditure will have to be covered by new borrowing. However, as income rises in response to increased expenditures, government tax revenues can also be expected to rise, with the result that the amount the government has to increase its borrowing from the public in order to finance the increase in its expenditures. Initially, virtually all the new expenditure will have to be covered by new borrowing. However, as income rises in response to increased expenditures, government tax revenues can also be expected to rise, with the result that the amount the government has to borrow each quarter to maintain its expenditure program diminishes over time. Initially, net new borrowing required to cover the deficit associated with the increase in expenditure of $100 million is likely to be about $90 million. At the end of six quarters, after tax revenues have been bolstered by the induced response in GNP, about $55 million in net new issues is required to cover the deficit associated with the change in fiscal policy. Given these estimated changes in net new issues, it is feasible to calculate the effect on interest rates of the assumed changes in fiscal policy from our estimates of the determinants of interest rates. And having derived estimates of the implied change in interest rates, one can proceed, as in the previous section on monetary policy, to estimate what offsetting effects these interest-rate changes have on the level of GNP and the balance of payments, with and without exchange-rate adjustments. A summary of these estimates is shown in Table VI. Corresponding estimates for a $100-million decrease in personal income taxes are shown in Table VII. The figures labeled "minimum estimates" in both tables are based on the assumption mentioned earlier that Canadian interest rates are linked to U.S. interest rates via expectations. On this assumption, according to our estimates, Canadian interest rates do not respond to changes in net new issues of government securities arising from changes in the government's deficit.

What conclusions can one draw from these figures? Considering only our best estimates, it is evident, first of all, that in the short run at least, the monetary consequences of fiscal policy changes for the balance of payments outweigh the expenditure effects. As a result, under a fixed rate the reserve position of the country would have improved; under a fluctuating system, the rate tended to appreciate. This conforms with Rhomberg's findings reported earlier. In the longer term, however, the expenditure effects of fiscal

TABLE VI

SIZE AND TIMING OF THE EFFECTS OF A $100-MILLION INCREASE IN GOVERNMENT EXPENDITURES ON GNP,
THE BALANCE OF PAYMENTS, AND EXCHANGE RATES
($ million)

	Quarters					
	1	2	3	4	5	6
1. Change in government deficit	90	85	81	71	63	55
2. Change in interest rates (percentage points)						
(a) Best estimate:						
long-term	0.055	0.052	0.050	0.043	0.039	0.034
short-term	0.074	0.070	0.067	0.058	0.052	0.045
(b) Minimum estimate:						
long- and short-term	0	0	0	0	0	0
(c) Maximum estimate:						
long-term	0.066	0.062	0.059	0.052	0.046	0.040
short-term	0.108	0.102	0.097	0.085	0.076	0.066
A. Without exchange-rate adjustments						
3. Change in GNP						
(a) Best estimate	101	105	113	130	151	171
(b) Minimum estimate	105	111	124	144	168	191
(c) Maximum estimate	100	102	110	126	146	166
4. Change in the balance of payments						
(a) Best estimate:						
current account	−25	−24	−29	−43	−59	−73
capital account	53	50	48	42	37	33
total	28	26	19	−1	−22	−40
(b) Minimum estimate	−26	−26	−32	−47	−64	−80
(c) Maximum estimate	70	66	57	33	10	−13
B. With exchange-rate adjustments						
5. Change in GNP						
(a) Best estimate	77	81	91	115	144	173
(b) Minimum estimate	119	126	144	174	211	248
(c) Maximum estimate	56	58	66	88	113	140
6. Change in exchange rate (cents)						
(a) Best estimate	0.2497	0.2376	0.1882	0.0682	−0.0545	−0.1648
(b) Minimum estimate	−0.1430	−0.1430	−0.1760	−0.2585	−0.3520	−0.4400
(c) Maximum estimate	0.4542	0.4269	0.3725	0.2362	0.1011	−0.0286

	Quarters					
	1	2	3	4	5	6
1. Change in government deficit	92	88	84	76	69	62
2. Change in interest rates (percentage points)						
(a) Best estimate:						
long-term	0.056	0.054	0.051	0.046	0.042	0.038
short-term	0.076	0.072	0.069	0.063	0.057	0.051
(b) Minimum estimate:						
long- and short-term	0	0	0	0	0	0
(c) Maximum estimate:						
long-term	0.067	0.064	0.062	0.056	0.051	0.045
short-term	0.110	0.106	0.101	0.091	0.083	0.074
3. *Without exchange-rate adjustments*						
A. Changes in GNP						
(a) Best estimate	51	49	51	56	64	71
(b) Minimum estimate	55	56	63	72	83	93
(c) Maximum estimate	50	47	49	53	60	66
4. Change in the balance of payments						
(a) Best estimate:						
current account	−25	−21	−23	−29	−33	−38
capital account	55	52	50	45	41	37
total	30	31	27	16	8	−1
(b) Minimum estimate	−26	−23	−26	−33	−39	−45
(c) Maximum estimate	73	72	67	53	41	30
B. *With exchange-rate adjustments*						
5. Change in GNP						
(a) Best estimate	26	22	24	31	39	47
(b) Minimum estimate	69	69	79	95	112	129
(c) Maximum estimate	−22	−24	−29	−36	−41	−47
6. Change in exchange rate (cents)						
(a) Best estimate	0.2576	0.2626	0.2342	0.1667	0.1152	0.0574
(b) Minimum estimate	−0.1430	−0.1265	−0.1430	−0.1815	−0.2145	−0.2475
(c) Maximum estimate	0.7422	0.6939	0.6733	0.6535	0.6296	0.6058

Source: Caves and Reuber, *Capital Transfers, op. cit.*, Tables 8.5 and 8.6.

policy outweigh the monetary effects on the balance of payments, leading respectively to a worsening of the reserve position of the country or to depreciation of the exchange rate. This longer-term picture, therefore, agrees with the conventional view of the adjustment process. It is also noteworthy that, if interest rates in Canada are closely geared to U.S. rates via expectations, our picture of the adjustment process conforms with the conventional view of the adjustment process in both the short and the long term.

A second important conclusion indicated by Tables VI and VII is that under a fluctuating rate the effectiveness of fiscal policy is considerably reduced relative to its effectiveness under a fixed-rate system, except in the situation where interest rates in Canada are linked to U.S. interest rates and are insensitive to changes in fiscal policy. This result is evident from a comparison of lines 3 and 5 in each table. Comparing our best estimates, one observes that this impairment is particularly serious in the case of tax changes. The effectiveness of changes in government expenditure policy is quite substantially reduced in the short run by exchange-rate variations, but after a year and a half the effectiveness of expenditure policy changes is about the same whether exchange rates vary or not. The difference in the degree of impairment sustained through exchange-rate variations by government tax and expenditure policies reflects the difference in the effects on the government deficit of these two types of policy changes. The cost to the government, in terms of the size of its deficit, is greater for a tax change, because of the associated additional leakage through savings on the first round of expenditure, as compared to a dollar-equivalent expenditure change.

The estimates summarized in Tables VI and VII bear on a central issue in the theory of economic policy: given a change in fiscal policy, to what extent do the changes in GNP associated with induced changes in exchange rates wipe out changes in GNP attributable to the net employment effects not associated with exchange-rate movements? In principle, it is conceivable that these counteracting influences might simply cancel each other out because of capital flows that are infinitely elastic with respect to interest rates and highly inelastic vis-à-vis exchange-rate movements. Empirically this theoretical possibility did not occur in Canada during the 1950s because, among other things, capital was less than infinitely elastic and capital flows did respond to exchange-rate movements.

A third general conclusion indicated by Tables VI and VII concerns the extent of the exchange-rate adjustment implied by the assumed changes in fiscal policy. Our estimated adjustments are substantially less than those suggested by Rhomberg's work. Given a $100-million increase in government expenditures during the 1950s, the immediate effect, according to our best estimate, was an exchange-rate appreciation of $0.0025. At the end of a year the rate may have appreciated by $0.0074. Thereafter the rate began to depreciate and after six quarters may have been $0.0052 higher than it was initially. The implied variations in the exchange rate for changes in tax policy were somewhat different. The impact effect was a depreciation of $0.0026; at the end of a year the rate had depreciated by $0.0092, and after a year and a half by $0.0109.

C. RESPONSES TO DEBT-MANAGEMENT POLICY

Since changes in the average term to maturity of the public debt affect GNP through changes in interest rates, the analysis of the effects of changes in debt-management policies is quite similar to that for changes in monetary policy. Table VIII presents a summary of the estimated effects of reducing ATM by ten months. These estimates were derived following the same procedure as was described earlier in connection with monetary policy. Only the best estimates are given in Table VIII.

As one would expect, the general results indicated by our estimates for changes in debt-management policy are somewhat similar to those for monetary policy. Exchange-rate adjustments greatly increase the effectiveness of debt-management policy in the short run—even more than they increase the effectiveness of monetary policy. In subsequent periods exchange-rate adjustments continue to enhance the leverage of debt-management policy, though less dramatically than in the short run.

In considering Table VIII, it should be recognized that a change in ATM of ten months represents a very substantial change in debt-management policy judged on the basis of the quarter-to-quarter changes which occurred historically during the period 1951–62 (with the notable exception of the Conversion Loan of 1958). It is also interesting to note that, in terms of its effect on long-term interest rates, a decrease of ten months in ATM is roughly equivalent to an increase of 1 percent in the rate of growth in the money supply. On this basis one can say, after comparing the figures summarized in Tables V and VIII, that irrespective of whether exchange rates adjusted or not, monetary policy exercised substantially greater leverage on GNP in Canada during the 1950s than debt-management policy.

3. Capital flows and economic policy

Evidence such as that presented in the preceding section is, of course, necessarily subject to a number of limitations which we acknowledge but do not propose to elaborate upon here.[10] Instead we focus our attention on the

[10]These are discussed in detail in Caves and Reuber, *Capital Transfers, passim.*

TABLE VIII

SIZE AND TIMING OF THE EFFECTS OF A DECREASE IN THE AVERAGE TERM TO MATURITY
OF THE PUBLIC DEBT BY TEN MONTHS
($ million)

	Quarters					
	1	2	3	4	5	6
A. *Without exchange-rate adjustments*						
1. Change in GNP	0.2	0.1	0.2	0.2	0.2	0.2
2. Change in the balance of payments						
(*a*) Current account	−0.1	—	−0.1	−0.1	−0.1	−0.1
(*b*) Capital account	−32.2					
(*c*) Total	−32.3					
B. *With exchange-rate adjustments*						
3. Change in GNP	24.6	1.4	3.0	4.7	5.4	5.4
4. Change in exchange rate (cents)	−0.2538	—	—	—	—	—

Source: Caves and Reuber, *Capital Transfers, op. cit.*, Tables 8.9 and 8.10.

central issue with which this chapter is concerned: To what extent did mobile capital flows enhance or diminish the effectiveness of the major instruments of stabilization policy? And related to this, what are some of the implications of highly mobile capital flows for the strategic design of an optimum stabilization policy?

Table IX presents a summary of the evidence reported in the preceding section on the responses in GNP to changes in fiscal, monetary, and debt-management policies, with and without exchange-rate adjustments, given the degree of capital mobility that prevailed during the period. The table also shows what the responses in GNP would have been had there been no capital flows. A direct comparison of these estimates indicates the degree to which the instruments of Canadian economic policy during the decade ending in 1961 were strengthened or weakened by capital flows and what effect exchange-rate adjustments had on the leverage of these policy instruments.

The figures showing the responses in GNP without capital flows are necessarily less reliable than those showing the responses with capital flows. They have been estimated using econometric techniques which essentially assume that, in the absence of capital flows, everything else would be roughly the same as it is when capital flows are highly responsive to policy changes. Such an assumption may be justified if we are concerned only with differences in marginal conditions. It is much more questionable, however, when we recognize that the assumption of no capital responses may imply far-reaching effects that have not been adequately allowed for in our estimates. In other words, instead of comparing the effects of capital flows on policy leverages on the assumption that everything else is more or less unchanged, it might be

TABLE IX

SUMMARY OF ESTIMATED EFFECTS ON GNP OF CHANGES IN FISCAL, MONETARY, AND DEBT-MANAGEMENT POLICIES WITH AND WITHOUT FOREIGN CAPITAL FLOWS AND WITH AND WITHOUT EXCHANGE-RATE ADJUSTMENTS ($ million)

	Without exchange-rate adjustments						With exchange-rate adjustments					
	1	2	3	4	5	6	1	2	3	4	5	6
1. Increase in government expenditure of $100 million												
(a) Without foreign capital flows	97	98	103	117	136	154	110	111	120	143	173	202
(b) With foreign capital flows	101	105	113	130	151	171	77	81	91	115	144	173
(c) b as a percentage of a	104	107	110	111	111	111	70	73	76	80	83	86
2. Decrease in personal income tax of $100 million												
(a) Without foreign capital flows	47	43	42	44	49	54	60	54	55	62	71	80
(b) With foreign capital flows	51	49	51	56	64	71	26	22	24	31	39	47
(c) b as a percentage of a	109	114	121	127	131	131	43	41	44	50	55	59
3. Increase in rate of growth in money supply of 1 percent												
(a) Without foreign capital flows	8.6	5.6	8.7	8.5	7.9	7.8	9.7	6.4	10.1	10.4	10.3	10.8
(b) With foreign capital flows	4.3	3.3	5.0	4.9	4.5	4.4	63.8	7.1	13.1	17.1	18.8	19.0
(c) b as a percentage of a	50	59	57	58	57	56	658	111	130	164	183	176
4. Decrease in the average term of the public debt by 10 months												
(a) Without foreign capital flows	3.9	2.3	3.6	3.5	3.3	3.3	4.5	2.7	4.2	4.4	4.4	4.6
(b) With foreign capital flows	0.2	0.1	0.2	0.2	0.2	0.2	24.7	1.5	3.3	4.9	5.6	5.5
(c) b as a percentage of a	5	4	6	6	6	6	549	56	79	111	127	120

Source: Caves and Reuber, *Capital Transfers, op. cit,* Table 8.11.

more appropriate to compare the effect of capital flows on policy leverages on the assumption that capital flows affect the basic structure of the economy. Our estimating procedures do not lend themselves to an analysis based on this alternative approach. Accordingly, the estimates of the responses of GNP to policy changes without capital flows shown in Table IX are necessarily somewhat tentative and can perhaps best be viewed as illustrative of the influence of capital flows on responses to policy changes.

It is evident from Table IX that capital flows substantially impaired the effectiveness of Canadian fiscal policy during the 1950s, when Canada adhered to a flexible exchange rate. The impact effects of fiscal policy changes were especially undermined; and the effectiveness of tax changes was considerably more impaired than the effectiveness of tax changes in government expenditures. The impact effectiveness of tax changes was reduced by 57 percent, and after a year and a half the effectiveness of such changes was still some 40 per cent less than it would have been without capital flows. The impact effect of changes in government expenditures was reduced by 30 percent, and after a year and a half, by 14 percent. Capital flows would have had exactly the opposite effect if Canada had fixed her exchange rate. The leverages of changes in government spending would have been increased some 4 percent in the short run and over 10 percent after a year and a half. The leverages of tax changes would have been increased about 10 per cent in the short run, and almost a third after a year and a half.

The effect of capital flows on the leverages of monetary and debt-management policy is naturally somewhat similar and is exactly the reverse of the effect of capital flows on the leverages of fiscal policy. Given a flexible exchange rate, capital flows enormously increased the impact effects of monetary and debt-management policies on GNP. And with a brief exception of two quarters for debt-management policy, this advantage was sustained on a lesser scale over the next year and a half. Under a fixed rate, on the other hand, capital flows would have reduced the leverage of monetary policy on GNP by between 40 and 50 percent and would have virtually emasculated debt-management policy as an instrument of stabilization policy.

The policy changes that have been assumed in constructing Table IX are entirely arbitrary and cannot simply be equated to evaluate the relative effectiveness of monetary, fiscal, and debt-management policies under different capital-market and exchange-rate conditions. In order to make such a comparison, it is necessary to consider not only the leverages of various policy instruments but also the "cost" of implementing policy changes. The cost of policy changes means different things to different people. For some it seems to mean mainly the trouble and subjective disutility of revising established habits of thought and practice. However, in the modern theory of economic policy, referred to at the outset of this chapter, "cost" is defined specifically as the degree to which the achievement of other policy objectives is impaired because of policy changes that move the economy closer to a particular objective that is in conflict with the fuller achievement of these other objectives. For example, assuming that governments regard low interest rates as preferable to high interest rates, one cost of tightening monetary policy in order to stabilize GNP is the increase in interest rates which the tightening of monetary policy is likely to entail.

In our work we have not attempted to evaluate the opportunity cost associated with the use of different policy instruments in the sense just described. Some information has been developed, however, which is relevant to this issue and which may be briefly considered.

First, as noted earlier, the assumed changes in monetary and debt-management policy are roughly equivalent in terms of their effect on long-term interest rates. On this criterion, the figures show that monetary policy is much more effective in regulating GNP than debt-management policy, irrespective of whether capital is mobile or not and whether exchange rates are adjustable or not.

A comparison of the amount of GNP created per unit change in interest rates, exchange reserves, and exchange rates is shown in Table X for expansionary changes in fiscal, monetary, and debt-management policy under different assumptions about capital flows and exchange-rate adjustments. If costs are reckoned in terms of long-term interest rates, it is evident that expansionary fiscal policy leads to interest-rate increases and that expansionary monetary and debt-management policies lead to interest-rate reductions. Thus, it is not feasible to compare the efficiency of fiscal policy with that of the other two instruments; some amount of either fiscal or monetary and debt-management policy will always be preferable, depending on the nature of the policy problem. Within the realm of fiscal policy, however, expenditure changes are always considerably more efficient in both the short and the long run than changes in tax policy, irrespective of whether capital flows are responsive or whether exchange rates adjust.

Another way of reckoning the cost of policy changes might be on the basis of the stability in interest rates, irrespective of whether changes in rates are positive or negative. On this basis, changes in expenditure policy are the most potent instrument in both the short and the long run, followed by changes in tax policy, which in turn are followed by changes in monetary and debt-management policies.

Turning from the opportunity cost of policy changes defined in relation to interest rates to an alternative definition of cost in terms of foreign-exchange reserves or rates, one finds quite a different pattern, depending on

TABLE X
GNP PER UNIT COST IN TERMS OF CHANGES IN INTEREST RATES AND IN FOREIGN-EXCHANGE RESERVES OR EXCHANGE RATES ASSOCIATED WITH CHANGES IN FISCAL, MONETARY, AND DEBT-MANAGEMENT POLICIES, WITH AND WITHOUT CAPITAL FLOWS[a]

	Impact effects				Cumulative effects after six quarters			
	Without exchange-rate adjustments		With exchange-rate adjustments		Without exchange-rate adjustments		With exchange-rate adjustments	
	GNP created per unit change in:		GNP created per unit change in:		GNP created per unit change in:		GNP created per unit change in:	
	l-t i.r.[b]	f.e.r.[c]	l-t i.r.[b]	f.e.r.[d]	l-t i.r.[b]	f.e.r.[c]	l-t i.r.[b]	f.e.r.[d]
1. Increase in government expenditures								
(a) Without foreign capital flows	+92	−4	+	−83	+145	−0.7	+	−16
(b) With foreign capital flows	+184	+4	+	+31	+63	+2	+	+34
2. Decrease in personal income taxes								
(a) Without foreign capital flows	+44	−2	+	−48	+51	−0.4	+	−1
(b) With foreign capital flows	+91	+2	+	+10	+25	+0.7	+	+5
3. Increase in the rate of growth in the money supply								
(a) Without foreign capital flows	−8	−4	−	−83	−8	−0.5	−	−12
(b) With foreign capital flows	−5	−0.06	−	−10	−6	−0.05	−	−3
4. Increase in the average term of the public debt								
(a) Without foreign capital flows	−10	−4	−	−83	−8	−0.5	−	−12
(b) With foreign capital flows	−8	−0.006	−	−10	−8	−0.006	−	−2

[a]Unit changes in interest rates are defined as 0.1 percentage points, unit changes in exchange reserves as $1 million, and unit changes in exchange rates as 0.1 cents. Plus signs indicate that an increase in GNP is associated with an increase in interest rates, an accumulation of reserves, or an appreciation in the exchange rate; minus signs indicate the opposite association.

[b]Long-term interest rates.

[c]Foreign-exchange reserves.

[d]Foreign-exchange rates.

Source: Bunton Capital Transfers on cit. Table 8.12

whether capital is assumed to be highly mobile or not. In relation to reserve losses or exchange-rate depreciation, an expansionary policy, whether through expenditure, monetary, or debt-management policy, is about equally efficient without capital flows, and tax policy is less efficient. With capital flows the efficiency of monetary and debt-management policies is greatly reduced on this criterion. On the other hand, when capital flows are introduced into the picture, expansionary changes in fiscal policy result in an increase in reserves or an appreciation of the exchange rate. As before, this means that it is not feasible to compare the efficiency of expansionary fiscal policy with the efficiency of expansionary monetary and debt-management policies. As between the two branches of fiscal policy, changes in expenditure are more efficient than changes in taxes, given highly mobile capital flows.

If, as in the case of interest rates, one measures the opportunity cost of policy changes in terms of *changes* in reserves or exchange rates, regardless of sign, fiscal policy—particularly expenditure changes—are more efficient than either monetary or debt-management policy.

The foregoing estimates of the efficiency of various instruments of stabilization policy, while interesting and useful, are much too simple to provide the basis for designing an optimum strategy for stabilization policy that would be very useful. In order to proceed with this task, one would need to introduce more policy objectives into the picture and specify and estimate in a more comprehensive and realistic way the opportunity costs of using the instruments of policy. But such a program would extend well beyond the boundaries of this study.

4. Integrated Capital Markets: A Review of the Implications for Stabilization, Growth, and Commercial Policy

The mention of economic integration usually raises visions of free trade areas, customs unions, and the like—multilateral changes in commercial policy to reduce the artificial barriers to the integration of national commodity markets. Sometimes national restrictions on migration, and thus labour-market integration, are removed or greatly modified at the same time. National capital markets may also attain varying degrees of integration with one another.

However, a significant degree of integration can occur, in national commodity markets, labour markets, or capital markets, without there being any formal free trade arrangement or similar mechanism between the countries whose economies are intertwined. In regard to capital markets, the degree of integration may be high or low by virtue of characteristics of financial markets themselves—the extent of full knowledge of lending and borrowing opportunities abroad, the availability of channels for easy and inexpensive international capital transactions, and the level of subjective fears concerning the risks of foreign borrowing and lending. The degree of financial integration may also be influenced by public policy: the U.S. Interest Equalization Tax on the yields of foreign securities is an example of a policy designed to reduce international financial integration.

This study deals with the very considerable, though largely informal, financial integration that exists between the capital markets of Canada and the United States, concentrating on the period of the flexible exchange rate. Most of our work may be summarized in answers to the following three questions.

1. What was the degree of financial integration between the capital markets of Canada and the United States from 1952 to 1961?

2. When changes in capital flows to Canada occurred, prompted by events outside the country or fortuitous changes in circumstances within the country, how much of a problem did these changes pose for Canadian economic policy?

3. How was the operation of Canadian domestic economic policy hampered or assisted by capital flows?

In this chapter the answers we have developed to these questions are briefly reviewed. In addition, in order to round out the discussion and relate it to other features of capital-market integration—as well as to other studies in the PPAC's Atlantic Economic Studies Program—some attention is given to the implications of highly mobile international capital flows for economic growth and for the integration of national markets for goods and services under free trade. We ourselves have not examined these latter aspects of the subject at any length; our comments are intended only to highlight some of the questions that arise in these areas and to note some of the empirical evidence bearing on these questions that has emerged from the work of other investigators.

1. Degree of integration between capital markets in Canada and the United States

Measuring the degree of capital-market integration by the responsiveness of capital flows to changes in interest-rate differentials, we confirm the prevailing view that financial markets in Canada and the United States are very closely but not perfectly integrated. In quantitative terms, during the period we have examined a 1 percent change in Canadian short-term interest rates, *ceteris paribus*, called forth a corresponding change in short-term capital flows in the same quarter of about 8 percent; and a 1 percent change in long-term interest-rate differentials evoked a change in long-term capital flows of roughly 10 percent in the same quarter.

A further manifestation of the high degree of integration that prevails between financial markets in Canada and the United States is the important influence that U.S. interest rates seem to have on Canadian rates via expectations. The evidence suggests that Canadian expectations about future long-term rates in Canada are closely linked to long-term rates in the United States —more closely than to expectations about future short-term rates in Canada.

It has proved more difficult to ascertain the responsiveness of direct capital investment to changes in differential rates of return between the two countries. There is some relatively weak evidence suggesting that direct capital flows are responsive to changes in long-term interest differentials, but much less so than both short-term capital flows and long-term portfolio flows: the elasticity coefficient is about 1.4. Strong evidence was found of a positive association between changes in direct investment flows and changes in Canadian GNP, which probably reflects both a cause and an effect relationship. For the most part, changes in direct investment flows appear to be much less closely geared to the variations in general credit conditions, as reflected in interest rates, than other types of foreign investment. They seem to be more closely related to developments in particular industries (such as the resource industries in the 1950s), the level of corporate liquidity, the rate of capital formation in new plant and equipment, and the prospects for direct investment in other parts of the world.

Further evidence on the close but imperfect integration between Canadian and U.S. financial markets is provided by the evidence on the responsiveness of capital flows to exchange-rate movements. During the period of the flexible rate, investors acted as if they strongly expected that any change in the exchange rate would be reversed—buying Canadian assets when the Canadian dollar fell and selling them when it rose. In the case of short-term capital flows, a 1 percent depreciation in the rate was typically associated with a simultaneous increase of some 70 percent in short-term inflows and an increase on the order of one-third in long-term capital flows within one quarter of the initiating change in the exchange rate.[1] An important consequence of this response pattern was that capital flows tended strongly to stabilize the exchange rate during the period when Canada adhered to a flexible rate.

2. Adjustment to capital inflows

Under the flexible exchange rate, exogenous increases in the various categories, of capital inflows—direct investment, portfolio investment, and short-term capital flows—tended to raise expenditure in Canada, reduce expenditure in the lending country, and elevate the price of the Canadian dollar to the extent that these income changes failed to reduce the current-account balance by as much as the initial disturbance raised the capital-account balance. Our investigation of these income effects of capital-flow disturbances in Canada has consisted of two parts: the effect of capital-flow changes on Canadian expenditure and the effect of Canadian expenditure changes on the balance of payments.

Our evidence indicates that, during the flexible-rate period, disturbances in foreign capital flows were fairly readily accommodated by the current account without requiring major policy or exchange-rate adjustments or significant disturbances in the rate of capital formation out of domestic savings. With full employment in Canada, an upward shift in the level of direct investment would generate an equal and opposite current-account shift within four quarters, after which the change in capital transfers would be "overrequited" and the Canadian dollar would tend to depreciate. With less than full employment, however, income changes in Canada associated with direct investment changes induced only about two-thirds of the required adjustment in the current account, and an exchange-rate appreciation was

[1] No evidence was found of an association between exchange-rate variations and direct investment flows.

required to complete the adjustment. Portfolio and short-term capital flows generated smaller income effects and thus were underrequited by much larger margins.

To this there is an important qualification when an increase in portfolio inflows was caused by a reduction in U.S. and other foreign long-term interest rates. The changes in the Canadian long rate observed in association with changes in the U.S. long rate are far too large to be explained solely by the accompanying change in international capital flows. This appears to reflect the strong expectational force described earlier: the Canadian rate is what it is because it is expected to maintain a roughly constant relation to the U.S. rate. In this case, disturbances in the flow of portfolio capital are associated with much larger changes in the Canadian interest rate than otherwise and are much more nearly requited by expenditure changes.

The other question raised in this connection is whether the current-account responses to simultaneous and past capital-account disturbances tended to offset the impact of that quarter's capital-account disturbance. The evidence suggests that during the flexible-exchange-rate period the income adjustment mechanism triggered by exogenous capital inflows helped to stabilize the impact of the inflows on the exchange rate.

3. The influence of capital flows on domestic policy
The third question that we have explored in considerable detail concerns how capital flows alter the effectiveness of the major instruments of stabilization policy—monetary, fiscal, and debt-management policies. The answer to this question depends to an important degree on whether one assumes a fixed or a flexible exchange rate. Consider fiscal policy first.

An increase in government expenditures or a reduction in taxes gives rise to an increase in GNP. Interest rates tend to rise simultaneously if the money supply is held constant, and this, in turn, induces an inflow of foreign capital, given highly integrated international capital markets. With a fixed exchange rate this induced inflow of foreign capital dampens the increase in interest rates, compared to what it would have been in the absence of capital flows, and consequently enhances the leverage of fiscal policy on GNP. During the 1950s, according to our estimates, the effectiveness of expenditure policy would have been increased by capital flows by about 5 percent almost immediately and by about 10 percent within a year of the initiating change in policy. The effectiveness of tax policy would have been increased by about 10 percent immediately and by about 30 percent within a year.

With a flexible exchange rate, capital flows have exactly the opposite effect. As capital inflows increase in response to higher interest rates, the exchange rate appreciates, thereby impairing the expansionary expenditure effects of changes in fiscal policy. Our estimates indicate that, during the period investigated, capital flows reduced the impact effect of changes in expenditure policy by about 30 percent and the longer term effect (within a year and a half of the change in policy) by about 15 percent. The impact effect of changes in taxes was impaired by almost 60 percent, and the longer term effect by some 40 percent.

The influence of international capital flows on the effectiveness of monetary and debt-management policies is opposite to its influence on the effectiveness of fiscal policy. In the absence of exchange-rate adjustments, the leverages of monetary and debt-management policies on GNP depend on the responsiveness of GNP to changes in interest rates and on the responsiveness of interest rates to changes in the money supply and the term distribution of the public debt. As monetary and debt-management policies become easier, interest rates tend to decline, thereby stimulating domestic expenditures. How much interest rates decline is conditioned in large measure by the mobility of international capital. Indeed, if international capital flows are completely elastic with respect to interest-rate differentials, domestic interest rates will remain unchanged, and monetary and debt-management policies have no direct effect on expenditure. The evidence for Canada suggests that, had the country adhered to a fixed-exchange-rate policy during the 1950s, capital flows would have diminished the effectiveness of monetary policy by between 40 and 50 percent compared to its hypothetical effectiveness in the absence of responses in capital flows. And the effectiveness of debt-management policy would have been reduced by substantially more.

A flexible exchange rate creates a new channel—exchange-rate adjustments—whereby changes in monetary or debt-management policy can influence domestic expenditure. As a result, international capital flows enhance rather than diminish the leverages on GNP of monetary and debt-management policies. As capital leaves the country in response to downward pressures on domestic interest rates, the exchange rate depreciates, the current account becomes more favourable, and this in turn strongly reinforces the expansionary effects that lower interest rates have on domestic expenditures. Our estimates indicate that Canada's flexible rate made the initial impact of monetary policy on GNP about six and one-half times as great as it would have been in the absence of capital flows; a smaller but still considerable margin of advantage remained after a year and a half. The impact effect of debt-management policy was enhanced by about five and one-half times.[2]

[2]Regardless of whether one assumes capital mobility or not, both monetary and fiscal policy apparently were much more effective in Canada under a flexible exchange rate than they would have been under a fixed rate.

Summing up, one may say that international capital mobility considerably increases the leverages of some types of stabilization policy and substantially reduces the leverages of other types, depending on whether the exchange rate is fixed or allowed to change freely in response to market forces. Thus, foreign capital flows have not so much altered Canada's ability to pursue independent stabilization goals as they have conditioned the manner in which the various instruments of policy need to be deployed to achieve these goals most effectively.

A related question concerns the degree to which Canadian monetary conditions are independent of U.S. monetary conditions. Our evidence indicates that no less than a fifth and no more than three-quarters of any change in U.S. interest rates was passed on to Canada in the absence of offsetting actions by Canadian monetary authorities. Our best estimate is that about 60 percent of the change in U.S. rates was transmitted to Canada. Turning the question around, one may ask what was the percentage loss in the independence of Canadian interest-rate policy because of capital flows: for long-term rates, our estimates suggest a loss in independence of about 40 percent, and for short-term rates, a loss of about 55 percent.

All the foregoing remarks on the influence of capital flows on the effectiveness of the instruments of stabilization policy, and on the degree of monetary independence that Canadians enjoy, are subject to an important qualification related to interest-rate expectations in Canada. As noted earlier, the evidence suggests that expectations about future long-term rates in Canada are considerably influenced by the current level of long-term rates in the United States. When allowance is made for this factor, our findings are modified in several respects, since in this situation interest rates in Canada are highly unresponsive to changes in Canadian policy. As a consequence, international capital flows are also much less responsive to changes in Canadian policy, and the differences in the leverages of policy, depending on whether or not one assumes adaptations in capital flows, are less than the foregoing estimates suggest. At the same time, the consequences of adhering to a fixed or a flexible exchange rate are also altered appreciably, since the pressures exerted on the rate by capital flows relative to current-account pressures are considerably reduced. Finally, to the extent that expectations about interest rates are closely governed by U.S. rates, the scope for monetary independence in Canada is greatly reduced, approaching the minimum estimates cited above.

4. Economic growth

The easy flow of foreign capital through integrated international capital markets in response to financial incentives opens the possibility of inducing foreign capital flows to serve the long-run growth objective of the community. If we abstract from such unlikely situations as hoarding the proceeds, spending them on current consumption, or substituting them for domestically financed investment, capital inflows are associated with some increase in the borrower's capital stock and some gain in output. Moreover, because various other factor inputs are associated with, or embodied in, imports of foreign capital, the effect of capital inflows on economic growth is probably substantially greater than simple consideration of the economy's over-all capital/output relationship alone would suggest. Among these ancillary factors are access to technology, marketing, and management skills, an increased capacity to bear risks, access to new and cheaper supplies of credit and materials, and cheaper access to new markets. Of course, all these factors must be compensated by income and dividend payments abroad. Theoretically it can be demonstrated that, given a set of fairly conventional assumptions, capital inflows speed the rate of growth of Canadian national income as long as the marginal productivity of capital exceeds the rate of interest paid for it (generally, its marginal cost).[3]

To what extent the benefits of foreign investment are, in fact, realized by local residents depends on a number of circumstances. In part it depends on the efficiency and effectiveness of local tax laws and administrations in appropriating a share of the profits of foreign investment for local use. In part, too, it depends on whether the local economy is sufficiently competitive to appropriate some of the gains of investment through lower prices. And finally, in part it depends on how important are the various indirect costs of foreign investment that have frequently been referred to, such as the stifling of export sales, the distortion of imports, and the covert repatriation of profits through phony intracompany pricing practices.

We have not attempted to shed any empirical light, in this study, on these aspects of foreign investment.[4] The only attempt that has been made, using advanced analytical techniques, to evaluate the effects of foreign investment on GNP indicates that, under the full employment conditions prevailing at the time, *net* foreign investment (imports minus exports) in Canada from 1950 to 1956 had added about 3¼ percent to Canadian GNP in 1956.[5] The contribution by gross foreign investment was somewhat greater. Any such

---

[3]This issue is briefly discussed in Caves and Reuber, *Capital Transfers and Economic Policy: Canada, 1951–62*, Cambridge, Mass., Harvard University Press, 1970, chap. 1.
[4]For a discussion of some of these questions, the reader is referred to *Foreign Ownership and the Structure of Canadian Industry, Report of the Task Force on the Structure of Canadian Industry*, Ottawa, Queen's Printer, 1968, and A. E. Safarian, *Foreign Ownership of Canadian Industry*, Toronto, McGraw-Hill, 1966.
[5]Rudolph G. Penner, "The Benefits of Foreign Investment in Canada, 1950 to 1956," *Canadian Journal of Economics and Political Science*, XXXII, May 1966, 172–83.

estimate is, of course, based on a variety of simplifying assumptions that necessarily qualify the result.

5. Commercial integration

So far, we have considered only integration in financial markets and its significance for Canadian economic policy. Commercial and financial integration are necessarily related, however. What effect would commercial integration—say, through the formation of a free trade area between Canada and the United States—have on capital movements?

The study of the effects of North American free trade by Ronald and Paul Wonnacott shows that, if the price of a Canadian dollar were no more than one U.S. dollar, the net impact of removing both Canadian and U.S. tariffs would be a net movement of manufacturing industry towards Ontario and Quebec.[6] If no changes occurred in capital flows, this net movement would lead to an improvement in Canada's trade balance, and to a tendency for the equilibrium price of the Canadian dollar to rise, while the adjustment was taking place. Some combination of currency appreciation with rising money wages in Canada would eventually limit the tendency for North American manufacturing to swing towards central Canada.

The significance of this shift for capital movements is that long-term foreign investment (direct and portfolio) would tend to increase in association with the expansion of Canadian manufacturing facilities. External financing would be a major source of funds, rather than a diversion from other lines of activity in Canada. Other sectors in Canada would feel pressure on their labour supplies, but not particularly on their access to funds to finance expansion. The total expansion of Canadian real gross domestic product would be greater than without this source of financing. The effect of international capital flows in this swing of North American manufacturing towards Canada would then be either to speed the adjustment or to let it continue without undue inflationary pressure in Canada.

Such induced capital inflows would also alter the expected behaviour of the balance of payments. The changing pattern of manufacturing location towards Canada, taken by itself, would improve Canada's trade balance and drive up the equilibrium price of the Canadian dollar (or otherwise limit the shift in manufacturing location). If capital inflows were "underrequited," they would also tend to improve the Canadian balance of payments and strengthen the tendency of international factors to slacken or limit the transfer of manufacturing towards Canada. On the other hand, "overrequited"

[6]Ronald J. Wonnacott and Paul Wonnacott, *Free Trade Between the United States and Canada,* Harvard Economic Studies, No. 129, Cambridge, Mass., Harvard University Press, 1967, pp. 182–8.

transfers would tend to worsen the Canadian balance of payments and deter the action of this set of checks on the manufacturing process. In this imaginary adjustment process, it is probable that capital inflows would primarily take the form of direct investment and that conditions of full employment would prevail. Our research on capital inflows to Canada during the 1950s and early 1960s suggests that they would be overrequited in these circumstances, and the tendency for the balance of payments to improve because of increasing net exports of manufactures would be mitigated. On the other hand, if the capital inflows are overrequited, this means that, on balance, they contribute to domestic inflationary pressures.

To summarize this rather complicated matter, the speed and the total size of the shift of manufacturing towards Canada that would ensue from North American free trade tends to be limited by two sets of factors: aggregate-demand pressures in Canada and upward pressure on the equilibrium price of the Canadian dollar. The transitional effect of capital inflows is definitely to relax the first limiting factor, and probably to relax the second as well. But to the extent that it relieves pressure on the balance of payments, it is less helpful for domestic aggregate-demand balance.

What effect free trade would have on capital flows in the long run, after the adjustment of industry to the absence of trade impediments had been completed, is somewhat less clear. As far as the demand for capital is concerned, it is conceivable that free trade, giving rise to new investment possibilities not related to the relocation of industry and the higher real income resulting from free trade, might result in an increase in the marginal productivity of capital independent of the shift associated with the transition to commercial integration. At the same time, as the Wonnacotts suggest, the advent of free trade might well considerably reduce the capital-output ratio in many Canadian industries. This tendency, combined with the increase in real Canadian incomes attendant on free trade, implies an increase in domestic saving relative to the value of new capital formation desired by producers. Thus, abstracting from any long-term effects of free trade on the marginal productivity of capital, domestic savings would rise relative to the demand for capital, and free trade in the long run would cause a reduction in the net inflow of foreign capital relative to Canadian income.[7]

[7] *Ibid.*, p. 187.

RELATED PUBLICATIONS BY THE
PRIVATE PLANNING ASSOCIATION OF CANADA

CANADIAN TRADE COMMITTEE PUBLICATIONS

THE WORLD ECONOMY

The World Economy at the Crossroads: A Survey of Current Problems of Money, Trade and Economic Development, by Harry G. Johnson, 1965.
The International Monetary System: Conflict and Reform, by Robert A. Mundell, 1965.
International Commodity Agreements, by William E. Haviland, 1963.

CANADA'S TRADE RELATIONSHIPS

Canada's International Trade: An Analysis of Recent Trends and Patterns, by Bruce Wilkinson, 1968.
Canada's Trade with the Communist Countries of Eastern Europe, by Ian M. Drummond, 1966.
Canada's Role in Britain's Trade, by Edward M. Cape, 1965.
The Common Agricultural Policy of the E.E.C. and Its Implications for Canada's Exports, by Sol Sinclair, 1964.
Canada's Interest in the Trade Problems of Less-Developed Countries, by Grant L. Reuber, 1964.

CANADA'S COMMERCIAL POLICY AND COMPETITIVE POSITION

Prices, Productivity, and Canada's Competitive Position, by N. H. Lithwick, 1967.
Industrial Structure in Canada's International Competitive Position: A Study of the Factors Affecting Economies of Scale and Specialization in Canadian Manufacturing, by H. Edward English, 1964.
Canada's Approach to Trade Negotiations, by L. D. Wilgress, 1963.

CANADIAN-AMERICAN COMMITTEE PUBLICATIONS

CANADA-U.S. ECONOMIC RELATIONS

Constructive Alternatives to Proposals for U.S. Import Quotas (a Statement by the Committee), 1968.
U.S.-Canadian Free Trade: The Potential Impact on the Canadian Economy, by Paul Wonnacott and Ronald J. Wonnacott, 1968.
The Role of International Unionism in Canada, by John H. G. Crispo, 1967.
A New Trade Strategy for Canada and the United States (a Statement by the Committee), 1966.
Capital Flows between Canada and the United States, by Irving Brecher, 1965.
A Possible Plan for a Canada-U.S. Free Trade Area (a Staff Report), 1965.
Invisible Trade Barriers between Canada and the United States, by Francis Masson and H. Edward English, 1963.
Non-Merchandise Transactions between Canada and the United States, by John W. Popkin, 1963.
Policies and Practices of United States Subsidiaries in Canada, by John Lindeman and Donald Armstrong, 1961.